THE
BRAIDED RUG
BOOK

THE BRAIDED RUG BOOK

CREATING YOUR OWN AMERICAN FOLK ART

NORMA M. STURGES

Lark Books

Dedicated to

Ed

Dori, Ed, Betsy

Amy, David, Megan, Nick, Katie, Jim, and Rebecca

Editor: Deborah Morgenthal
Art Director: Kathleen Holmes
Photography: Michael Drejza
Illustrations: Caroline Cleaveland
Manuscript Typist: Susan Stewart
Production: Elaine Thompson and Kathleen Holmes

Library of Congress Cataloging-in-Publication Data
Sturges, Norma.
    The braided rug book : creating your own American folk art / by
Norma Sturges.
       p.   cm.
    Includes bibliographical references and index.
    ISBN 0-937274-91-7
    1. Rugs, Braided.   I. Title.
TT850.S87   1995
746.7'3--dc20   95-14990
                                                             CIP

Published in 1995 by Lark Books
Altamont Press
50 College Street
Asheville, NC 28801

© 1995, Altamont Press

10 9 8 7 6 5 4 3 2 1

Every effort has been made to ensure that all the information in this book is
accurate. However, due to differing conditions, tools, and individual skills,
the publisher cannot be responsible for any injuries, losses, and other
damages which may result from the use of the information in this book.

CONTENTS

Acknowledgements

▼ ▼ ▼

I would like to give credit to my husband Ed for all his years of support and whose idea it was to write this book. To my daughter Betsy Sturges-Murray for helping with the book in so many ways. To my granddaughter Amy Kupko for her help with early shows, and to Jane and George Sturges for their assistance and encouragement.

I would also like to thank Tangy Buchanan, who arranged my rugs in the family-owned, Stewart-Buchanan Antiques, and who recommended Mike Drejza as a photographer. Thanks to Mike, too, for appreciating braided rugs and for his photos. Also thanks to Cynthia Pasquale, *The Denver Post Home Style* magazine editor, for her article, and to their photographer Lyn Alweis.

Many thanks to Susie O'Brien for writing my brochure. To the Ken Caryl writer's group for their encouragement—especially Susan Stewart who did my letters and typing, and who was a sounding board as I went along. To Caroline Cleaveland, a former student, who did my illustrations.

Thanks to the owners of Quilts In The Attic for inviting me to teach these last 12 years, and to Audrey Fisher, Director of Adult Education at Arapahoe Community College, for appreciating braiding and so asking me to teach for many years.

Craft people build on one another—and so my thanks to braiders who have published their works. My appreciation to my students for their encouragement and to those whose rugs are a part of this book. Thanks, too, to the braiders in the gallery of this book whose rugs serve to inspire.

Lastly, my thanks to Rob Pulleyn, publisher of Lark Books, who realized that a braiding book was needed—and chose mine. To Deborah Morgenthal, the editor, who has been a joy to work with—this book is a reflection of her expertise and style. To Kathy Holmes, the art director, and the many others who contributed to the book—my deepest appreciation!

Maxwell Mays, *Country Kitchen*

I believe in cord wood, iron stoves, and breakfast
I believe in freshly baked bread and mail order catalogues,
ticking clocks, dogs and cats and corn right out of the garden.
I believe in families who laugh together and because of this
I believe in tomorrow and the day after and the goodness of man
and the joy of living.

Maxwell Mays

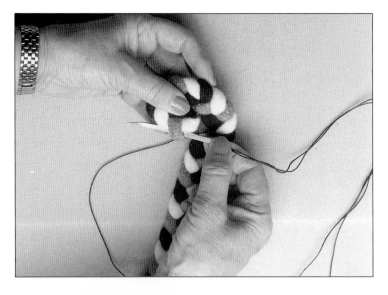

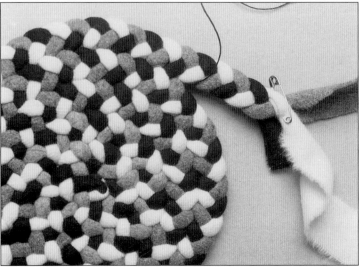

Top: Lacing the *T* on a circle rug.

Middle: Getting ready to change colors

Left: All loops laced to butt last row

SUBJECT OF THE BOOK

Since 1830, American families have treasured their braided rugs. They are a symbol of hearth, home, comfort, family, and love. The braided rug is a unique American craft. This book includes a brief history, illustrated with historic photographs. The book offers instructions and color designs for braiding your own rugs. In addition, you'll find a gallery of rugs created by some of the country's best braiders.

Many grandmothers made braided rugs, but few taught their craft. I'm the grandmother who is going to change that.

Sturges Family Christmas card, 1954

Introduction

▼ ▼ ▼

Braiding rugs is an American tradition that, as with many crafts, developed out of a need and developed into an art.

It was kept alive in the 20th century to enrich homes with a timeless quality, compatible with decor of many styles.

A braided rug is a satisfying personal, artistic expression, and may well turn out to become an heirloom, passed on from generation to generation. Above all, a braided rug is an object of beauty, with the unmistakable warmth, richness of texture, and depth of color that only pure wool, braided with care, can deliver.

Technically, a braided rug is three *strands* of wool, with their edges turned in, joined by repeatedly pulling the right *tube* to center position and then the left—just the way you braid hair. The *continuous braid* is then *laced*, or sewn, together.

In the early days of braiding, old clothing was used to make rugs. Today, any type of fabric or fiber can be used, but the strength of wool makes it the best choice for a long-wearing rug.

Wool coats with torn pockets or faded colors can be rejuvenated; colors come back to life after seams are opened and the coat is washed in the washing machine. Recycled in this way, the old wool faces a longer life than if it had remained a coat.

However, today's rug braiders usually don't have the time to take apart clothing. Fortunately, there are sources available for purchasing new, reasonably priced wool. The equipment needed is minimal: a clamp, lacing thread and needle, and probably Braid-Aids® (used to fold in the edges of the wool strands).

I have been braiding for more than 40 years, developing and refining my own style and technique along the way. Each of my rugs has been inspired by a unique need or vision, and, as such, is an integral part of my family's history and of my own development as a crafts person. I'm very possessive of my rugs. Each is interwoven with fond memories. Braiding also has served as an outlet for creative expression, providing me with a great deal of satisfaction.

My first attempt at braiding occurred while I was awaiting the birth of my first child, Dorie, now 45. I envisioned a cozy, old-fashioned nursery with a pink and blue braided rug.

Although I loved this rug for sentimental reasons, it really didn't turn out that well. I had no pattern, no teacher, and could find little information on how to turn my dream into reality. The following year, I attended the Eastern States Exposition, the fair for all of the New England States where the best of all aspects of New England country living are displayed. I was able to obtain a pattern and begin braiding in earnest.

Now I am the one teaching classes in rug braiding and demonstrating braiding at country fairs and crafts exhibitions. Although teaching is very rewarding, I wanted to find a way to encourage more would-be braiders. I'm certain that somewhere across the country there are many, many people eager as I was to make a braided rug but who lack the necessary information.

This book represents my desire to share braiding with a wide audience. The rugs and patterns you'll find here will allow you to create beautiful rugs for your home and family. The oval, round, and heart patterns come with complete instructions and can be executed in your choice of colors. Other rugs are presented in different sizes with individual color plans. For the adventurous, there are even hexagon, strip, three-circle, scalloped, rectangular, and watermelon rugs.

When you braid a rug by hand for a special place or person, you take part in the long tradition of making functional, one-of-a-kind works of art. The welcome rug (braided, of course) has been rolled out for you. I invite you to enter the world of braiding and find out how simple and satisfying this time-honored craft can be.

Opposite page: Janice Jurta, *New Hampshire Rug*,
4' x 6' (1.2 x 1.8 m) 3-circle

The braided rug is truly an American discovery— a *folk art*, made by "folks" nearly 170 years ago.

According to authors Jean Lipman and Alice Winchester (*The Flowering of American Folk Art 1776–1876*),

"Folk Art had some common denominators - independence from cosmopolitan, academic traditions; lack of formal training, which made for interest in design…a simple and unpretentious rather than sophisticated approach, originating more typically in rural rather than urban places and from craft rather than fine-art traditions."

Anyone who has family or friends who braid may recognize those characteristics in their rugs and in their creators.

Braiders today have the qualities consistent with Lipman and Winchester's definition of a folk artist of the previous century, that is, someone with "a sense of personal commitment to the work and of pleasure, even excitement, in carrying it out in a fresh, free way."

The Emergence of Braided Rugs as Floor Coverings

In the 1700s, early American homes had wooden floors covered with straw, corn husks, and rush woven mats. In 1750, the first carpets appeared, but only the very wealthy could afford these imports. Loom-woven rag carpets were made in the late 1700s. By 1816, painted floor cloths were very popular.

Although braided rugs are often associated with the colonial era, the craft did not develop until the early 19th century. Like three strands of wool braided together, there are three factors that account for the development of rug braiding: the popularity of braided straw bonnets and floor mats, an interest among homemakers in floor covering, and the introduction of local factories producing woolen fabric.

In the late 1700s, straw bonnets and floor mats were braided in Providence, Rhode Island and in the neighboring Massachusetts towns. This craft then spread to Maine. Many woman in these communities earned money braiding straw bonnets. By the early 1800s in New England, there were 24 "manufactories" producing woolen fabric, many of them in the same towns where straw braiding was done. Wool was now readily accessible in America and was favored for floor coverings because it was more durable than cotton or straw and more beautiful as well. The development of the power loom in 1839 made available commercially produced carpets. Manufactured rugs were too expensive to be purchased

Straw Hat Maker, Little Book of Early American Crafts & Trades

by the general public, but they did have the effect of heightening interest in attractive floor coverings. Thrifty, but clever, New England housewives, who already knew how to braid, were inspired to create a new craft for their homes: the braided rug.

The earliest braided rugs date from the 1820s in New England. During this time, homemakers started experimenting with many types of rug, including braided, hooked, embroidered, needlepoint, yarn sewn, and shirred. According to Sally Clarke Carty (*How to Make Braided Rugs*), the first recorded braided rug was made by a Miss M. Locke of Andover, Massachusetts. She won two dollars at the Essex Agriculture Show in 1827 for her rug that the judges described as a "very pretty braided rag rug."

The craft continued to proliferate throughout the 19th century; as Americans traveled across the prairies in covered wagons during the westward expansion, they transported a few treasured possessions—including their braided rugs. In fact, these rugs became the pioneers' primary floor coverings.

In the early 20th century, the braided rug enjoyed an upsurge of interest; widely promoted by interior designers and the new, upscale home magazines, braided rugs were praised as purely decorative items, rather than as an inexpensive way to cover floors. Showcasing intricate shapes and the color pallet of the day, braided rugs achieved a design height never again equalled.

From the 1960s through the 1970s, the braided rug lost some prestige and fell outside the mainstream of design; as a result, expert rug braiders became a rarity. Fortunately, as we approach another century, braided rugs are rapidly resuming their original function as items with a dual attraction: they are beautiful and they fulfill a real need.

Perhaps their greatest appeal for us today lies in their symbolism, in that they evoke images of a simpler era when home, family, and friends were unchallenged as the central elements of our lives.

The Wallace Nutting Connection

Wallace Nutting was an American minister who retired in 1904 at the age of 44 and turned his prodigious talents to taking photographs, collecting antique furniture, making reproduction furniture, restoring vintage homes, and writing. It is for his photography and writing that we braiders are grateful; his photographs of the interiors of colonial homes, published in his States series books titled *Beautiful Connecticut*, *Beautiful Massachusetts* (and New York, New Hampshire, Maine, Vermont, Pennsylvania, and Florida) captured for posterity the enduring beauty of braided rugs.

During his photographic period, it is said that he took 50,000 scenes in New England, Europe, and the Near East. He reproduced 1,000 different photographs millions of times. By 1936, ten million Nutting photographs had been sold. Most of his New England photographs were of apple blossoms, streams, stone walls, country lanes, and homes. Fortunately, he also took many interior photos, arranged by his wife, of great New England colonials, showing the furniture and decor of the early 1900s. A wide variety of braided rugs are showcased; there are medium-sized scattered braided rugs, very large, room-sized braided rugs, and many interesting shapes that are rarely seen today. For instance, a photograph he took in the Webb house in Withersfield, Connecticut shows a very large, sophisticated rug with nine circles combined to make one rug.

He generally decorated the rooms with ovals and circles of various sizes. These shapes, then and now, are by far the most popular. His photograph called "The Quilting Party" has a three-circle braided rug on the floor. This rug inspired me to make my own three-circle rug, called "Heather Roses" (page 79).

Several of his photographs show women, dressed in colonial clothing, braiding rugs. The technique for the rug shown in the Rug Maker on page 14 was to keep braiding until you had a large pile of braid and then sew the braid

1930s ten-strand braided rug with swirl effect

Above: Wallace Nutting,
The Rug Maker

Left: Wallace Nutting,
The Quilting Party

into a rug. We call this a *hit-or-miss* type rug. It was as popular then as it is today.

Nutting articulated his philosophy on floor coverings in *Connecticut Beautiful*: "One may mix the braided and the hooked rugs, or the hooked and Turkish rugs, but braided rugs form too strong a contrast with Oriental rugs. Large rugs are more desirable by far. The effect of many patches is bad."

In 1904, he and his wife, Mariet Griswold, bought a beautiful farm in Southbury, Connecticut and named it Nuttinghame. This farm was his headquarters for eight years. Photographs of his home reveal a collection of braided rugs. One of his most famous interiors, shown below, was his own living room at Nuttinghame. He photographed it so many times and sold so many of these images that he said his living room paid for the farm.

His appreciation of braided rugs aside, my interest in Nutting is personal, as well. My mother-in-law, then Eula Curtiss, was photographed by him in 1909 wearing colonial period dress . Her picture, "Who's In the Parlor" (right), is one of the first interior photographs in his *Connecticut Beautiful* book. He photographed her in Woodbury, Connecticut in a home owned by her grandfather, Daniel Curtiss, who bought the house in 1834. The mirror she is looking into is also one of my family's treasured possessions.

Fred Thompson of Portland, Maine and David Davidson of Providence, Rhode Island also photographed in the same period and region, using the same technique—black and white photographs, hand-painted by women colorists. Braided rugs feature prominently in their photographs, too. We are fortunate to have this pictorial record to document the appeal braided rugs had for early Americans.

Above right: Wallace Nutting, *Who's in the Parlor?*

Right: Wallace Nutting, *Proposing an Amendment to the Linen*

Braided Rugs as a Shaker Craft

The Shakers, whose formal name is the United Society of Believers in Christ's Second Appearing, are a religious sect founded by Ann Lee, an English factory worker. She and her eight followers came to America in 1774. After years of persecution and hardship, the sect, at its peak in the 1840s, grew to about 6,000 members in 18 separate communities. The Shakers believed they could experience God and His love directly, and that in their striving for perfection, they could live as if the kingdom of heaven were already manifest on earth. They practiced equality of the sexes, separation from the world, hierarchy of authority, and celibacy. Hard work was also a tenet of the Shaker religion. Author Beverly Gordon (*Shaker Textile Arts*) quotes Mother Ann, as Ann Lee was called, telling her followers to "put your hands to work and your hearts to God."

This philosophy and their cloistered lifestyle produced communities distinguished by fine craftsmanship in their buildings, furniture, baskets, and textiles. They also invented much of the equipment used in their everyday life. The Shakers were encouraged to keep journals to record their time and ideas. Their sales and purchase records were also preserved so that we know that in 1838, in Watervliet, New York, they made 40 dozen braided sashes for sale.

Starting in 1840, the Shakers made impressive rugs of many types: braided, crocheted, hooked, shirred, and knitted. It was in their rugs that the Shakers could express their love of color and design; in their rugs, their creativity could blossom.

The Shakers made brightly colored braided rugs with small, tight braids. Their braids were plaited (a flat braid with the fold on the back), and they laced the rows together by lacing every other loop. They made the usual three-strand braid but also did up to a seven-strand braid. They made interestingly shaped rugs, such as the eight-scalloped rug below.

The Shakers also had a strong sensitivity to color and blended colors subtly, alternating dark and light rows in concentric rings. They loved borders and used borders within borders. In fact, braided borders became a recognizable Shaker trademark. This design element was practical as well as beautiful, because braid is strong and protects the edges of a rug.

The Shaker Museum in Chatham, New York houses three outstanding examples of Shaker rug making: circular, made from brightly colored dyed yarn, they are flat-knitted in bands that are butted or joined together. Their elaborate patterns and design give an Aztec or Indian appearance. These rugs are also bordered by up to three to four rows of braid—either a three- or five-strand braid. Another of these knitted circular rugs is in the collection of Robert Booth; on the back of the rug is written, "Made 1892 by Sister Elvira in her 88th year." These rugs are truly remarkable works of art that haven't been surpassed to this day.

Shaker scalloped braided rug, Hancock Shaker Village Collection, Pittsfield, Massachusetts. Photographer: Paul Rocheleau

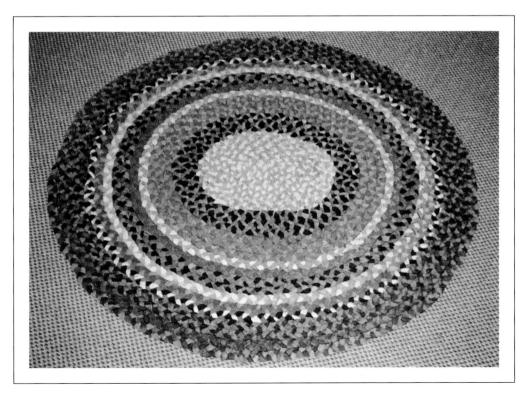

Above: Shaker knitted rug with braided border, Shaker Museum, Chatham, New York

Right: Shaker braided rug, Shaker Museum, Chatham, New York

Beginnings — A Scrapbook

▼ ▼ ▼

My family moved to Woodbury, Connecticut, a beautifully preserved colonial town, when I was in my early teens. It was a peaceful village of picturesque homes filled with antiques, braided rugs, and other examples of family crafts.

"Antiques are what link this generation to those before," I have heard. I believe this is also true of crafts such as rug braiding.

Whenever I demonstrate, people always come up to me and wistfully say, "I remember my grandmother, mother, or father braiding." Often I can detect in people the desire to carry on the tradition of braiding. But they don't know how to take that first step.

All braiders have stories about the first rug they made, or about braided rugs they have saved, or about those that got away. Every braider has to make a first rug. It may not turn out to be a showpiece, but it is treasured because it represents a courageous plunge into something new.

Here are a few of my favorite stories about beginners and the special rugs they bravely created.

Old Sparhawk

When I first started braiding in 1949, I saw a rug I thought was the most beautiful I could imagine—9-by-12-feet (2.8 x 3.7 m) with wonderful colors. I talked to the people at the Old Sparhawk Mill in Portland, Maine where the rug was

made, and they sent me a pattern. One of my first students, Doris Newell, made it for her living room. Doris loved to braid but didn't like to lace the braid together. So she would braid and braid, and I would go over, almost on a daily basis, sit on the floor, and lace a round or so. (I don't lace on the floor anymore!) I made a smaller version for Ed, my then six-year-old son, to use in his knotty pine bedroom. This was one rug that did wear out; he also wore out his wooden bureau, so I didn't feel too badly.

A year or so ago, I got the urge to make a version of this same rug. It combines old red, maroon, light and medium green, medium blue, blue-gray, brown, black, gold, and beige. I've named this rug "Old Sparhawk" in honor of the mill that inspired me many years ago.

Jane Sturges and Her Mother, Ruth Platt

In 1955, I started teaching a few friends in Woodbury, Connecticut to braid. In the winter of 1957, my sister-in-law, Jane Platt Sturges, wanted me to teach a class at the Southbury Training School where she was a social worker. There were 22 in the class including her mother, her aunt, her cousin, her best friend, and many other personnel from the training school. We met all winter in the cafeteria. It was a great place with plenty of tables and good lighting. Some of these individuals made room-sized rugs. Jane's was quite distinctive—a circle with a tiny firm

braid. She started with shades of light blue and changed to dark blue in about seven rows, then switched to a light gold to dark orange/rust, then switched to greens and reds, following the same light to dark pattern. I photographed this rug after it had been on the floor for 35 years. Its colors are still perfect. However, with hard wear it flattened out—as flat as the hardwood floor it sits on. It is a beautiful one-of-a-kind rug, as are all individually designed rugs.

Jane's mother, Ruth Platt, was an amazing woman. When we met, she was a widow caring for 15 retarded adults who lived in the wing of her large farmhouse. She was a wonderful cook; I still remember her sticky buns! She braided one rug and became so infatuated with the craft that she started selling rug wool out of her barn. Later, she turned the farm over to a daughter, bought an old colonial house in Woodbury, Connecticut and built a shop on the back. From the time she was 60 until she was 70, she sold rug wool and other fabric out of her Fabric Barn, as the shop was called. At the age of 81, she finished another rug. She made this 6-foot (1.8 m) hit-or-miss rug for her son.

A Salesman's Sample

In 1957 I made a salesman's sample rug. In those days, the woolen mills wove many yards of fabric for tailors, using every color combination they could weave. If the tailor wanted a certain color combination, he would cut a piece out of the wool and attach it to his order. Braiders sometimes were able to use what was left of the bolt.

This combination of beautifully blended wool made great rugs. My rug had a mosaic look to it, and I gave it to my sister-in-law, Jane. She has enjoyed it for the past 37 years, and it is just starting to show wear.

Reclaiming Dori's Rug

When my oldest daughter Dori was about eight, I made her a 6-by-8-foot (1.8 x 2.5 m) braided rug in dusty rose, pink, gray, beige, and camel to match her bedspread and curtains. It remained her bedroom rug through college when we sold our Massachusetts home.
I shipped the rug to her in Colorado for Amy, her five-year-old daughter. Amy's bedroom was small, but it worked well until baby sister Megan arrived to share her bedroom. Dori and her husband Buzz bought a larger house but didn't have a place for the rug. Dori agreed to let us borrow it. I brought it home and gave it a place of prominence on our bedroom floor. The taupe and dusty rose colors match our room perfectly, and I have enjoyed it on a daily basis ever since.

Ed and the Case of the Missing Rug

In 1978, we sold our great old New England colonial in Massachusetts and put our furniture in storage—except, of course, I took my braided rugs with me. We visited our son Ed in Connecticut for a few weeks and then came on to Denver. My husband Ed got a job in Vail, and our possessions were shipped there. When I unpacked, I realized the rug I was working on was missing. A few months later, my son moved to Vail, too; he drove out, followed closely by a truck carrying his furniture. We were waiting to help him unload when this large, open truck came into view with a 4-foot (1.2 m) braid flapping from the side. "Well, there's my rug," I said, with a mixture of relief and dismay. Dangling out was the gold, cream, and beige section of the rug. The 2,100-mile trip apparently didn't harm it. I cite this story when people wonder if braided rugs are fragile.

(Another common concern is how to clean them; this rug has never been cleaned and has been on the floor for 16 years.)

I call this rug "Aspen," as it is just the color of the gorgeous aspens we so enjoyed in Vail.

Our Christmas Card—1989

Every year I try to find Christmas cards with scenes that include braided rugs in the setting to send to friends. Sometimes I photograph my own. I call this my "Poinsettia" rug because the red is the exact shade of the red poinsettia. The rug uses my "Americana" pattern, substituting red and green for blue, gray, red, and plaid.

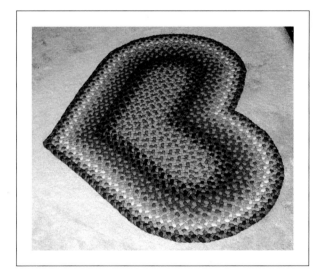

Home is Where the Heart is

When Ed married Jayne, I gave them the first heart rug I had made, and it has been by their bed or at the front door ever since. When I demonstrate, the heart seems to be the most admired rug.

A Peter Rabbit Rug for Bets

When my daughter Bets was planning her nursery, she and I bought pastel gingham and calico cotton to make a crib quilt. She wanted a Beatrix Potter theme, so I bought a Wedgewood lamp with Peter Rabbit in the briar patch and designed a rug from this lamp.

When her daughter Rebecca was little, she loved to creep on this rug, enjoying the texture and the many pastel colors. When she was about two-and-a-half years old, her mother explained to her that I had made the rug for her. When I came over, she said, "Grandma, you made this rug for me—thank you!" With delight, she realized that I had also made

the braided hit-or-miss rug in their front hall. Then she pointed to their oriental rug in the living room and asked, "And, Grandma, did you make this one, too?"

As it turned out, I had to make this nursery rug again; it became pretty awkward taking it off her nursery room floor every time I wanted to show it. It is 5-by-7 feet (1.5 x 2.2 m), and at an hour a day took me more than three months to make. The photographs of the rug's development show how the look changes with the addition of new colors.

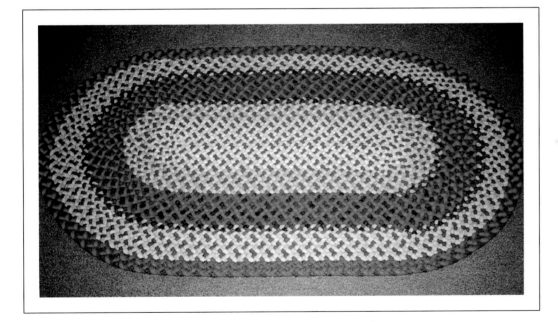

Men Do Braid

I haven't taught many men. Quite often they express an interest, but being the lone male in a class with ten women can be a challenge. One fellow met that challenge. Jim Armstrong does cable maintenance and installation repair for a telephone company. He loved braiding and would stop at thrift stores and tell me about the great blankets he found. Once he was sent to Wyoming for a special job. He packed his tool chest with wool and braided in the motel room in the evening. He got a bit of kidding from his buddies, but he held up. Jim has gone from this first rug to demonstrating the craft at local fairs and festivals.

Dr. Jim Delany, an obstetrician-gynecologist, wanted large rugs for his Colorado ranch and decided to make them himself. He found directions in a book and, with a little help from me, is now making beautiful rugs for his special setting.

A Quilter, Quilts, and Braided Rugs

Jean Erbe was in one of my first braiding classes in Denver. She is a gifted tapestry weaver and quilter. For her first project, she braided a rug from a wool blanket she had dyed many shades of mahogany. Later, she created a matching, quilted wall hanging.

Helen Nielsen and her husband Steve designed their rug to match a quilt. He ripped the strips and she braided. She was a mathematician and explained to me that the number of skips in each half of the ends of the rug should be equal to ensure a well-shaped rug.

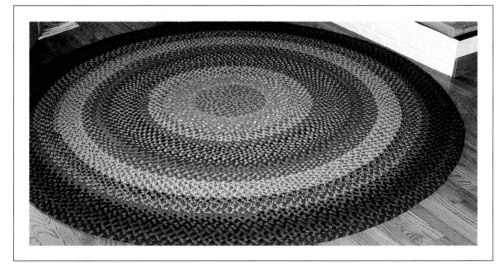

Complements and Compliments

Norma Watkins designed her rug to complement the country look she likes so well. The rug suits her cheerful, bright kitchen nook.

Glenda Moore has received many compliments on this first rug, which she called "Barnstable," designed for her Colorado mountain home.

Thinking Big

The largest first rug made by one of my students was Judy Hardje's 9-1/2-by-12-foot (2.9 x 3.7 m) rug shown here. It was for her family room.

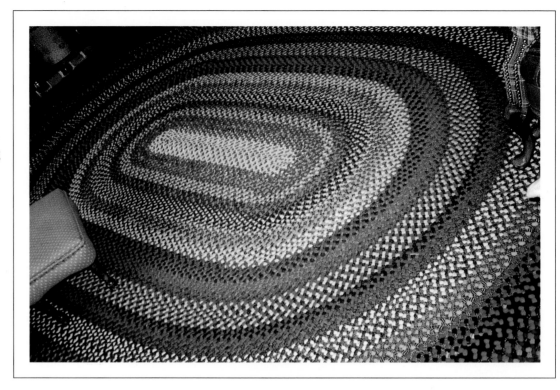

Robbie Mallin started braiding again to create this cheerful rug for her kitchen.

Kathy Zotowey makes the rugs and her husband makes the furniture. Quite an unusual combination of talents.

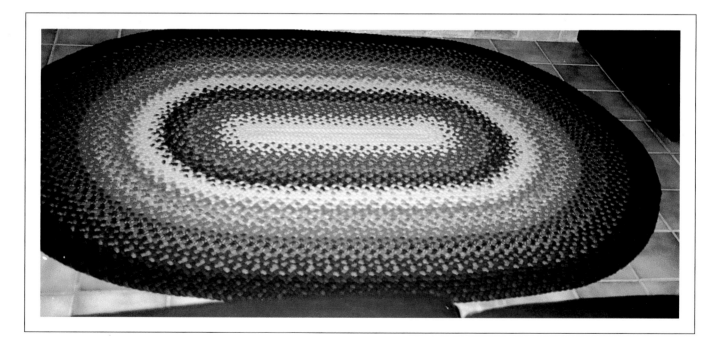

Many students make rugs for mothers, daughters, sons, aunts, cousins, brothers, and sisters. Shirley Harmon has made rugs for all of these relatives. This is one rug she kept for herself.

Joy Busch, a textile designer, is that rare beginner who has the skill, patience, and talent to tackle an advanced rug. She combined the two braiding techniques, a strip and a rectangle, and made it in a pattern. She did an amazing job.

All in the Family

We have many second generation braiders. Janet Spaulding took lessons because her 81-year-old mother, Ruby Putnam, could braid but no longer lace; they decided to work together. This is a rug her mother made in Woodstock, Vermont in about 1956. It is a perfect and very pretty rug.

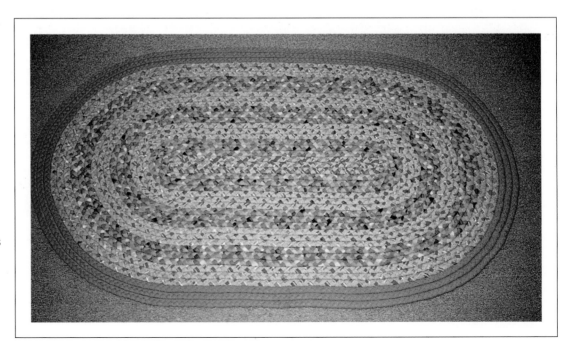

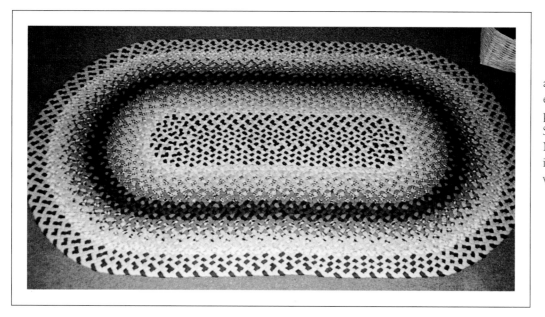

Marguerite Boyne has a rug for which her mother, Marie Stege, won first prize in the Minnesota State Fair 40 years ago. Marguerite and I examined the rug and decided we couldn't do better.

One last, very special rug was made by Miriam Dawson in Woodbury, Connecticut. Mrs. Dawson was the mother of Rachel Dawson Riefe, my best friend in high school and college. Miriam started braiding in the late 1940s. This rug was 34 years old when the photograph was taken. As you can see, the rug is beautifully braided, has great color choices, and is wonderfully preserved—a legacy to enjoy for many years to come.

I believe these examples show how braided rugs play a part in our lives and in the lives of our families and friends. As the rugs get passed to other generations, the beginnings start again.

Why Do People Braid?

People braid primarily to create a rug for a certain person or place. A homemade rug adds interest, sparkle, and warmth to a room.Children's books, television programs, and consumer magazines have kept the mystique of the braided rug alive by using them to denote comfort, home, and family. In Tasha Tudor's book, The Dolls' Christmas, the illustrator shows braided rugs in and in front of the dollhouse, under the childrens' Christmas tree, in the kitchen, under the cat in front of the living room fireplace, and next to the bed. In Mickey Mouse's house at Disney World, there is a braided rug in every room. Braided rugs are used occasionally in Norman Rockwell's paintings, in Disney's Peter Pan and Wendy books, and on the cover of the Mormon Family Home Evening. Grandma Moses used braided rugs in her illustrations for The Night Before Christmas, by Clement C. Moore.

One of my favorites uses of the braided rug in popular American art is a Maxwell Mays print of an old-fashioned kitchen, complete with three braided rugs and braided chair seats; it truly denotes a cheerful, happy kitchen.

A book editor who wanted a braided rug to photograph in front of a fireplace for a book on country Christmas commented, "What could be better than a braided rug in front of a fireplace to show the Christmas theme?"

Mary Randolph Carter, when referring to floor coverings in *American Family Style*, writes, "Hooked and braided rugs are what we love best."

We like the idea of coming home to warm, comfortable, meaningful furnishings: heirlooms, collections, quilts, and rugs made or collected by family members. These items are like icons that connect us with the values of the past; they're part of our roots.

My daughter Bets gave me a card saying, "happiness is homemade," our family motto.

So, why do people braid? I ask my students why they are learning to braid at the start of a new class. Here are some of their answers.

-They saw a rug or a demonstrator or an article that inspired them to try it.

-Their mother, father, or grandmother braided and they know the rugs last forever.

-They like to try a lot of crafts.

-They like "country."

-They collect antiques and think braided rugs go well with them.

-They have admired friends' or neighbors' braided rugs.

-It's a relaxing craft, good for stress relief.

-They like pioneer crafts.

-They have hardwood floors and want a rug for a certain place.

-One student bought a commercial rug for her son's bedroom. He is now one year old, and the rug is wearing out. Now she's braiding one that will last.

-A dental hygienist with two children and expecting another said, to my surprise, that she wanted something to do while waiting.

-Another student priced a braided rug and decided she was too "tight" to pay the price.

-A nurse who worked in a teen psychiatric center at night liked to braid during the long night hours.

-One student's uncle was an alcoholic and took up braiding when he quit drinking.

-Several students are braiding to decorate family cabins and ranch houses.

-Many make rugs for their own homes, then go on to fill requests from relatives and friends.

-They inherited their mother's wool and want to learn to braid, too. One woman called her first rug "My Turn."

So why do I braid? After making rugs for many years for our old colonial, then for family and friends, I now braid to see the great effects obtained by combining colors. I also enjoy the challenge of making interestingly shaped rugs.

If you fit into any of these categories or have reasons of your own and are ready to go— let's get to it!

Author at Beaver Creek, Colorado's annual folk art festival

Planning Your Rug

▼ ▼ ▼

The first thing you need to identify is the meaning behind the rug. Is it for a cozy nursery, family country kitchen, reading nook, first impression in the entryway, or is it a gift? You then interpret the desired image into decisions about size, color, and style.

Those decisions are primarily based on where you're going to put the rug. Is it a hard use area like in front of the kitchen sink, under the table, or in an entryway? If so, you need to be sure to use sturdy wool of medium to dark colors so that your rug will wear well and resist soil. If your goal is to create a rug for a light traffic area such as a bedroom, you can use pastels and white wool.

Do you want the rug to dominate the space or blend in? Use strong colors if you want it to be a focal point; solid colors tend to look brighter. If you want it to blend into the room, use subtle colors, gradual shading, and many strands of blender colors—grays, browns, camel, beige, and tweeds in every row. Blenders tend to soften the look of the rug. If you're not sure where the rug is going to be placed, just braid in colors you like or colors you wear and you will find a place for it.

My students usually make what I call "decorator rugs." They bring beautiful swatches of upholstery fabric, drapery material, or wallpaper to match to the wool. This shows us what their color needs are.

Planning the Size of Your Rug

The second reason for knowing where you plan on putting the rug is so you can measure the area and braid an appropriate size rug. The eventual size of the rug is governed by the length of your center row.

How do you get the right size if you are making an oval rug? The rule is *measure your space, subtract the width from the length, and add one inch for every foot.*

Here's an example: The space is 4 feet wide and 5 feet long (1.2 x 1.5 m). Subtract: 5 minus 4 = 1 foot plus 1 inch. The center braid needs to be 13 inches (33.5 cm) long. You calculate every size oval rug this same way. Here's a second example: You want a 9-by-12-foot (2.8 x 3.7 m) rug. Subtract: 12 minus 9 = 3 feet (92.5 cm) plus 3 inches (8 cm). The center braid needs to be 3 feet (92.5 cm), 3 inches (8 cm) long, or 39 inches (100 cm).

Planning the size of a circle rug is even easier. You start by braiding six *twice overs* (see the circle rug directions on page 59) and continue braiding until the rug is the right size.

I recommend starting small so you can get your technique under control. The 2-by-3-foot (62 x 92.5 cm) oval rug on page 39 is specifically designed for beginners.

Planning the Type of Rug

Beginner Level Rugs

Beginners should keep their color plans simple; don't use a great many color changes, unless you are making a hit-or-miss rug. This is so you will concentrate on your braiding and lacing. First make a flat, well-shaped rug and then get more creative on your next rug.

The easiest type of rug to make is to braid any one wool plaid in pleasing colors and use the wool for all three strands. This works well for a chair seat but may be a bit monotonous for a whole rug.

Hit-or-miss rugs are also easy. There are several types:

1. Add any color wool at any time.
2. Select wools that are predominately shades of one color, as in my "Bits 'N Pieces" rug on page 77 .
3. Carry one color in one strand throughout the rug. Use a second color for the second strand throughout the rug and randomly vary the color in the third strand.
4. Another easy plan is almost the same as the one above. Continue with one color per strand for two of your strands and vary the third. The difference is that instead of randomly changing the color in your third strand, you always change the color on the shoulder (as per oval directions, page 47). Coordinate your colors.

My "Bittersweet" rug on page 68 is an example of an easy-to-plan, standard shaded, 2-by-3-foot (62 x 92.5 cm) rug. It is comprised of five center rows of medium shades of wool, followed by three rows of lighter colored wool. These center colors are used again, then are gradually shaded into a darker border. To avoid having obvious color changes, you should change only one color at a time and change the color on the shoulder (see oval rug directions, page 47).

For the Advanced Braider

As an advanced braider, any number of color changes are fine. My "Country Heart" on page 65 used 15 different colors and shades of wool. If you want to change all three colors at the same time, you need to utilize the *butting* technique (page

51). In order to butt, you need to *rattail* your *continuous braid*, and then start a new braid that you butt or join together. By doing this you can change from solid red to solid blue as in my "Americana" rug, page 70.

One basic color rule: Don't place your darkest rows in the center or the rug will appear to have a hole in the center. Start your center with medium or light rows. If you start with medium- colored wools, you can shade lighter or darker. To shade lighter, take out your darkest wool strip and add a lighter strip. To shade darker, take out your lightest shade of wool and add a darker strip. Thereafter, alternate between the dark and the light bands.

I usually finish my rugs with a few rows of fairly dark wool. This frames the rug. If you like, though, you can end with medium or light rows; this tends to make your rug flow into the room. My "Victorian" rug on page 75 is one example of this look.

In my early days of rug braiding, I made monochromatic rugs. Monochromatic rugs always create a peaceful, blended look, and they are easy to design. One of our bedrooms was blue, so I made a predominately blue and grey rug. In the gold bedroom, I used many shades of gold, camel, beige, and rust (below). The rose bedroom rug is pictured on page 20. As you can see, I combined dusty rose, pink, camel, and gray. Two of my three early rugs have survived 30-something years of wear in "hard use" bedrooms. In our bedroom, we had green, blue, and gold wallpaper, so I became more adventurous and combined the three colors.

Students tend to make rugs that duplicate their teacher's "look." I try to encourage individuality and creativity, but this usually takes the experience of making a few rugs. It has always seemed harder to me to mix a lot of colors. When creating the "Nursery" rug, I bought a Beatrix Potter set of books and a lamp with Peter Rabbit in the briar patch and carefully studied the colors. My motto was if it's in the lamp, I can put it in the rug. On page 77, you can see how many colors I incorporated.

For the "Nantucket" rug (page 78), I did the same thing—found a picture and duplicated the colors. For the "Amish" and "Country Spring Heart" rugs (page 69 and page 71), I followed colors from quilts. My "Coals on the Hearth" rug (page 74) came about because I bought three long, heavy-weight wool skirts at a garage sale. I looked at the red, gray, black, and white plaids and thought they would make an interesting rug.

There are many good looking rugs in magazines and books that you can use for inspiration. If you like the rug, you can figure out approximately the color choices necessary to get the same look. Many times beginners can't translate their ideas into a color plan without a model to go by. The joy of braiding is in creating individual rugs. You need to enjoy the colors you are working with and the style you have chosen. It is only through trial and error that you will be able to judge what works for you.

Author's *Old Gold* rug, designed to match her daughter's bedroom.

Wool Talk

▼   ▼   ▼

Wool truly is the premium clothing fiber of all time, unmatched by today's man-made fibers.

Rug braiders have recognized wool's great qualities since the first braided rugs were made. Woolen rugs are soil resistant; vacuuming is all they usually need. They last almost a lifetime even in a hard use area. My 2-by-3-foot (62 x 92.5 cm) rug in front of the door from the garage is holding up better than the wall-to-wall carpet it sits on. My front hall braided rug has stood proudly for over ten years in that demanding place.

Wool is water repellent. When I wash wool in the washing machine, I have to push it down with a long wooden spoon to get it to absorb the water. Rug braiders also appreciate the fact that wool dyes beautifully, is flame resistant, and has great bulk.

Here are answers to the most commonly asked questions I hear about wool.

What is the best weight rug wool?

I recommend wool that is easiest to braid and wears the longest. One test is to fold the edges of a 1-1/2-inch-wide (4 cm) strip into the center and then fold the edges together again: does the strip make a nice, well-rounded tube?

Braiders often buy wool by the pound. Wool that weighs between 1 pound (454 grams) and 1-3/4 pounds (794 grams) per yard is preferable. If you don't have a scale handy, the best wool includes medium-weight coat wool, medium-weight blanket wool, and heavy-weight skirt material. Wool blends are fine as long as the weight is good. Sources for purchasing rug wool are listed on pages 110–111.

Why is the weight of the wool important?

Lightweight wool produces a rug with tweaks and folds in it. This results in a unattractive rug and one that is not totally reversible. You have to cut/rip lightweight wool into 2 or 3-inch-wide (5 or 7.5 cm) strips; this means extra folding which is more time consuming; it also doesn't wear as well.

On the other hand, heavy, stiff, or flat wool, like military uniforms, Melton cloth, heavy bonded wool, and heavy blankets, is generally hard to work with. It doesn't fold easily, is hard on the hands, and makes a larger braid. Men's worsted suiting is too lightweight and flat. Loosely woven tweeds need to be cut, won't wear well, and get caught in the Braid-Aids.

Why shouldn't I recycle old wool clothes?

If you are a beginner braider, resist the temptation to use every piece of wool you have. I know that our grandmothers did this, but I believe our tastes in decorating are not the same. Many rug books extol the virtues of using any old wool garment you own or see in thrift stores, but I have only had a couple of students interested in making rugs from used clothing.

My students have found that it takes longer to make a rug when they have to take apart the garment. Moreover, it takes a lot of practice to successfully work with the differing weights of wool recycled from a cashmere coat or plaid skirt.

I suggest that you start with wool that is easy to work with—60-inch-wide (152.4 cm), clean, new, ready to use wool. You then measure 1-1/2-inches (4 cm), snip, and rip from selvage to selvage to get a 60-inch-long (152.4 cm) strip ready to braid. This is a big time saver. Coat-weight wool usually has a fuzzy and a flat side. I almost always use the flat side, but this is just a personal choice. Using the fuzzy side makes the braid look larger. Helen Howard Feeley who wrote the 1957 classic, *The Complete Book of Rug Braiding*, preferred the fuzzy side.

Gauging the weight of wool is often hard for beginners. The solution is to braid practice strips. This will help you recognize when your braid is getting larger or smaller. As you get more proficient in your braiding, you can work comfortably with varying weights of wool by varying the width of your strip.

Should I precut or prerip the wool?

No. I know it is a temptation. It looks neat to have it all ready to braid. But every time you change colors and sew on a new piece of wool, the added strip has to make the same width braid. If all of your strips are precut, you don't have this option and this might limit your color choices.

What is a good width braid?

Measure from the top dent to the bottom of the loop. My braids are usually 7/8 inches (2.2 cm) wide. A few people

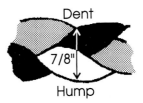

braid 3/4 inch (2 cm) to produce a small braid. Years ago, many rug makers braided a larger braid— up to 2 inches (5.5 cm) wide. It just depends on the look you want; it is a personal choice. The wider your braid, the more wool you use. With a wide braid, you have a heavier, thicker rug, and it braids up faster.

Some people think the larger braid looks more "country." Perhaps they do go well in rustic homes or ranches. I like "country" but I also have always made the smaller braid.

How much wool will you need?

A good rule of thumb is 2/3 pounds per square foot of rug; a 2-by-3-foot rug is 6 square feet times 2/3 = about 4 pounds of wool. The metric version of this formula is the area of the rug in square meters x 3.2 = the approximate weight of wool in kilos.

How do I take care of my rug?

This is often one of the first questions I'm asked. How would I clean it? I have only had one rug professionally dry cleaned. It is a possibility. Because wool is soil resistant, a thorough vacuuming takes care of dirt for the life of the rug. It is a good idea to turn your rugs over and around and also to use a rubberized mat or pad under the rug. This adds to the life of the rug. It is especially important to use a pad under a small rug so that it doesn't slip.

The American Wool Council has these recommendations for spot and stain removal:

Alcohol or food—place a towel under the area. Gently rub carbonated water toward the center of the spot over the stain.

Blood—blot with common starch paste and rinse from the back with soapy water.

Burning cigarette—brush off ash.

Butter and grease—sponge with a dry-cleaning solvent.

Chewing gum—scrape and sponge with a dry-cleaning solvent.

Chocolate—sponge with soapy water.

Coffee and tea—sponge with glycerine. If none is available, use warm water.

Egg—scrape and sponge with soapy water.

Glue—sponge with alcohol.

Ink—immerse in cold water.

Iodine—treat with cool water followed by alcohol.

Iron rust—sponge with a weak solution of oxalic acid until the stain disappears. Then, sponge carefully with household ammonia and rinse with water.

Lipstick—may often be erased by rubbing white bread over the area with a firm, gentle motion.

Mud—once dry, brush and sponge from the back with soapy water.

Tar and road oil—sponge with dry-cleaning solvent.

Wine, Red—immerse in cold water.

The above list enumerates major problems. I also use carpet spot remover. I take a toothbrush and brush the spot remover onto the stain; then I rinse well with cold water.

Cleaning with Water and Fresh Air

Usually the only problem with my braided rugs is an accumulation of soil from years of wear. If the rug needs an overall cleaning, or if there has been a recent accident, we put it on our porch chaise or picnic table and sponge with a mild liquid detergent. Then I turn the hose on to rinse the rug and let it dry outdoors. Once, we put a rug on our round picnic table to dry and the squirrels pulled up a couple of loops, so beware of squirrels.

Cleaning with Snow

For years I have heard people refer to cleaning their braided rugs in the snow. Judy Borger of Pottstown, Pennsylvania described the process so clearly that I tried it and was very pleased with the results. According to Judy, you need two or more inches (5 cm) of powdery snow. Roll the rug out on an untrampled area and stomp on all parts of the rug to pack the snow into every crack underneath. Turn the rug over onto another pristine snow area and sweep off the top of the rug (the swept snow should be dirty). Then stomp on all parts of the newly swept side. Continue turning, sweeping, and stomping until the swept snow is pure white. Judy says that the rug should not be wet if the snow is powdery, and can be put right back on the floor. I hung mine for a day to be sure it was completely dry.

Braided Rugs Are Meant For Floors

Rugs love to be on the floor; they thrive and survive. They don't hold up well if rolled up and left in dark places, especially if they have been used and not cleaned thoroughly before being put away. Moths and bugs get at them and chew away. A good moth spray helps if you are storing your rugs. Also, moth balls help preserve your wool.

What if I really want to recycle old wool?

Here are some tips if you can't resist taking wool clothing apart. I rip every seam, but I cut out the collar and hard-to-rip parts. These parts are usually too small to use anyway. After the garment is completely apart, I wash the pieces in the washing machine with cold water on the wool setting, using a little detergent made for washing wool. Then, I hang the pieces to dry. If hems and seams need ironing, use the wool setting and a pressing cloth. If your wool is lightweight or flat and needs to be made bulkier, try hot water and dry it in the dryer. Be careful of tweeds; wash them more gently (shorter cycle) or they will fray.

Be very selective in the clothing you take apart; for example, I never buy a bonded wool garment. Before you buy the garment or take apart your mother's old coat, ask yourself: Does it have a lot of seams? Is there a sewn-in belt? These things will shorten your strips and you will have a lot of waste.

I had two 1960s pleated skirts that looked almost the same; they weren't. One had three pieces including the skirt band and 11 ounces of usable wool. The other had 10 pieces, totaling 9 ounces of wool, and of course, a lot of wasted time and wool.

What other fabrics can I braid with?

People always ask about braiding with cotton. The technique is the same except you rip your strips wider. Making cotton rugs is not a satisfying craft for me. Cotton makes a firm, hard braid that is full of creases and tweaks; you are always battling the loose threads. Quilted cotton works okay; your bulk is sewn in. If you want to use cotton, I recommend that you crochet a rug.

Any fabric that has the same bulk or body as wool can be braided. One student was allergic to wool and made a good, colorful rug out of velour. Another student, Judith Felsburg, made a terrific rug out of denim to match her son's bedroom.

I started this chapter by saying that wool lasts almost forever. Take my watermelon rug for example. After searching for the right shade, I remembered a coat I had about 40 years ago that was in a chest in the basement. As you can see, it made a great watermelon.

I don't mean to discourage you from braiding old wool; it is fun using some wool you can identify as belonging to a family member or friend. Once I was told that my "Old Sparhawk" rug was lost in shipping. My response was, "Oh no, my father's bathrobe and son's Valley Forge pants are in it!" Recycled wool does present certain technical and design challenges, and you may want to make a first rug using new wool. Sometimes when I am demonstrating, people are surprised that one or several of the strands I am using came from coats I have taken apart. This appeals to people, especially when I demonstrate at historic places. They like the fact that we are still doing rugs the way they were done in the "olden" days.

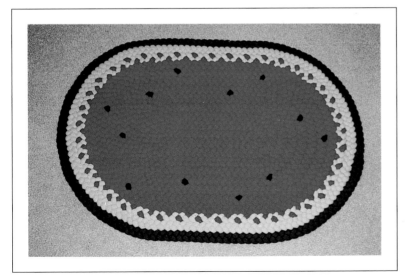

Above: Judith Felsburg's denim rug

Left: Author's *Watermelon*, made from an old wool coat

Getting Started
▼ ▼ ▼

You are now ready to start braiding. Rug braiding, like many crafts, is accomplished by using a number of specialized and general tools. If you are new to braiding, I recommend that you acquire the following items on the list below. You'll see that compared to other crafts, braiding requires very few gadgets. If you own a basic sewing machine and can use a needle and thread, you are off to a great start! At the end of this section on page 37, you'll find detailed instructions for building a rug braiding stand.

Basic Equipment

Table to attach Braid-Klamp to and to lace on

Sewing machine to attach strips

Braid-Klamp®

Vari-Folder Braid-Aids® (optional)

Braidkin® (lacing needle)

6-ply linen lacing thread (or)

Braided cotton splicing thread (or)

Beeswax nylon thread

1-1/4-inch (3.2 cm) T-pins or plastic-headed pins

6-inch (15.2 cm) metal ruler

Sharp dressmaker scissors

6 #2 safety pins

Sewing needles and matching thread

Medium-size tapestry needle - #18 or #19

Needle nosed pliers or hemostat

Loose-fitting glove with fingertips cut off for wearing on lacing hand (optional)

Rug braiding stand (optional)

General Rules for Easy Braiding

There are a few general rules to follow that really do make it easier to braid well.

First of all, find a comfortable place to braid. You will need to work at a large table. Sit in a comfortable chair and make sure you have good lighting.

Attach a clamp to the table or use a floor stand. A clamp does a good job of holding your braid while you work. Set up your sewing machine close to your work table. Although wool strips can be attached by hand, I find it quicker and the stitches tighter when I use a sewing machine. Last, but by no means least, always lace on a table or other flat surface.

Preparing Wool Strips

Prepare strips only when you are ready for them. Wool weight varies so much that it's important to have the flexibility of varying the width.

Rip the wool whenever possible. When ripping strips, use a metal ruler. Measure each strip carefully, cut a couple of inches and rip the rest. Check the width to make sure the wool is ripping straight. Tweeds sometimes need to be cut. When cutting, measure all along the wool to keep the width uniform.

When ripping or cutting wool, go from selvage to selvage or the length of the piece, whichever produces the longest strip.

My instructions say to cut or rip your strips 1-1/2 inches (4 cm) wide. This is for the best weight wool, coat weight. No two pieces of wool are the same. When you're starting a rug or changing colors, try one strip and check the look of the braid. The braid needs to remain the same width.

If you have only lighter weight wool, your strips should be anywhere from 1-3/4 inches (4.4 cm) to 2-1/2 inches (6.4 cm) wide. Lightweight wool (like skirt weight) tends to tweak. This means there are wrinkles in your braid. If possible, use only one strand of lightweight wool along with two strands of good weight wool at a time.

If you are a beginner, try to find the best weight wool so that the edges fold in easily. Advanced braiders can braid all types and weights of material.

My braids are approximately 7/8 inches (2.2 cm) wide, measuring from the dent on one side to the hump opposite it.

Basic Techniques

Instead of reading through a basic techniques section in

advance of the projects, you will learn all the techniques you need as you braid a complete rug.

We'll start with the oval rug, by far the most popular braided rug shape. This is a small rug--a good beginner size. We'll meander slowly and carefully through this project, stopping often to learn in detail how to execute all the elements that go into braiding a rug.

The second project is the circle rug; instead of repeating the basic techniques, you will refer to those steps in the oval rug. This rug is slightly larger than the oval.

The third and final project is for making a heart-shaped rug, a more difficult undertaking. Here again, you will refer back to the oval rug at key stages.

Before you begin the projects, read the glossary on page 109 so that you will recognize the braiding terms. Also, read the project instructions at least twice, and try to visualize and reason through all the steps. That way, you'll be familiar with the road we're going to take.

Whale Rug Braiding Stand

What You Need

(1) 3/4-inch-thick (1.9 cm) solid lumber or 3/4-inch (1.9 cm) plywood, 4 inches (10.2 cm) wide by 8 feet (2.5 m) long

Enlarge 123% for actual size

(1) 1/2-inch (1.3 cm) plywood, 3-1/2-by-8-1/2 inches (8.9 x 21.6 cm)

(1) 1/4-inch (0.6 cm) carriage bolt, 2-1/2 inches (6.4 cm) long

(1) 1/4-inch (0.6 cm) washer and wing nut

(1) 1/4 x 3-inch (0.6 x 7.6 cm) spring with two small screws

sandpaper

wood glue

varnish

paintbrush

What You Do

1. Crosscut the 3/4-inch (1.9 cm) stock to the following lengths: 33-1/8 inches (84.1 cm), 30-1/8 inches (76.5 cm), and 23-7/8 inches (60.6 cm).

2. Rip the 33-1/8-inch (84.1 cm) length at 2-5/8-inch (6.7 cm) width. The 30-1/8-inch (76.5 cm) piece stays the same width. Rip the 23-7/8-inch (60.6 cm) piece at 3-1/2 inches (8.9 cm).

3. Crosscut these three pieces to make the following measured pieces:

33-1/8-inch length = (2-5/8 x 29 inches) + (2-5/8 x 4 inches)[84.1 cm length = (6.7 cm x 73.7 cm) + (6.7 cm x 10.2 cm)]

30-1/8-inch length = (4 x 15 inches) + (4 x 15 inches)

[76.5 cm length = (10.2 cm x 38.1 cm) + 10.2 cm x 38.1 cm)]

23-7/8-inch length = (3-1/2 x 14 inches) + (3-1/2 x 9-3/4inches)

[60.6 cm = (8.9 cm x 35.6 cm) + (8.9 cm x 35.6 cm)]

5. Now take the two 4-by-15-inch (10.2 x 38.1 cm) pieces and make a right and left piece, as shown in the detail drawing. Make the four vertical dadoes approximately

3/8-inch (1 cm) deep and wide enough for a snug fit of the 3/4-inch (1.9 cm) material. Then mark and cut a 3/4 x 3-1/2-inch notch for the bottom 14-inch (35.6 cm) cross brace.

6. Assemble the base with glue, nails, or screws. There is no need to further secure the vertical staff.

7. Cut the whale out of your 1/2-inch (1.3 cm) lumber; sand off any rough edges. Notch the top of the staff.

8. Hold the whale against the top of the staff; mark and drill 1/4-inch (0.6 cm) holes through the top of the staff and the bottom of the whale. Mount the whale with the carriage bolt, being sure to put on the washer before screwing on the wing nut.

9. Drill a 1/4-inch (0.6 cm) hole 1 inch (2.54 cm) from the whale's bottom lip (about 1-1/2 inches (3.8 cm) from the carriage bolt) and 4-3/4 inches (12.1 cm) from the top of the staff. Attach the spring with the two small screws to create tension; when you push the whale's tail down (as shown in the drawing), the whale's mouth will move up to hold the braid in position. To release the tension on the braid, push the whale's head down. Loosen and tighten the carriage bolt to hold the whale in position.

10. Apply a coat of varnish to finish your stand.

Original design, Bill Lucas
Instructions and drawings, Richard Beauvais-Nikl

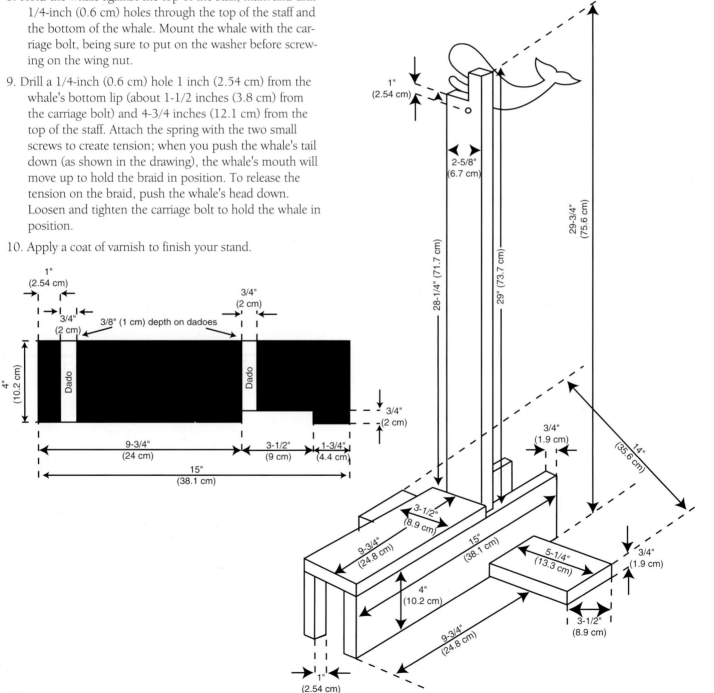

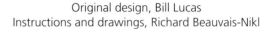

38

The Oval Braided Rug

▼ ▼ ▼

The oval rug is one of the easiest to make. It is the most popular shape, probably because it fits a great many areas. My "Country Spring Oval" (below) is 2 by 3 feet (61.5 x 92.5 cm), a good size for the beginner braider.

Calculating the Length of the First Row

To figure out the length of the first row, subtract the 2 foot width (61.5 cm) from the 3 foot (92.5 cm) length. This gives you 1 foot (31 cm). Add 1 inch (2 cm): the center braid is 13 inches (33 cm) long.

This is a standard design, going from medium shades in the center to darker bands, then some light, and ending with the darkest bands. Beginners may not want to include as many colors. Yellow, purple, and green could be eliminated and the look would be almost the same. This would leave six colors, a good number for the novice braider. Light gray could be substituted for white, making the rug more soil resistant.

How to Count Rows

Basic to braiding is knowing how to count rows. Here's how it's done:

The first 13 inches (33 cm)—or the distance to the twice overs—is Row 1. Row 2 is all the way around the center row. Row 3 and the following rows are a complete circuit of the rug.

Materials

The "Country Spring Oval" uses about 4-1/2 pounds (2.1 kilos) of wool, or 4 yards (3.7 m). Review the equipment listed on page 36. Make sure you have matching sewing thread.

Country Spring Oval

Rows 1-3	White	Med. Blue	Lt. Blue
Row 4	Dusty Rose	Med. Blue	Lt. Blue
Rows 5 & 6	Dusty Rose	Med. Blue	Blue Gray
Row 7	Dusty Rose	Med. Purple	Blue Gray
Row 8	Dusty Rose	Med. Purple	White
Row 9	Lt. Pink	Med. Purple	White
Row 10	Lt. Pink	Lt. Yellow	White
Row 11	Lt. Pink	Lt. Blue	White
Row 12	Med. Blue	Lt. Blue	White
Row 13	Med. Blue	Lt. Blue	Med. Green
Row 14	Med. Blue	Blue Gray	Med. Green
Row 15	Med. Blue	Dusty Rose	Dusty Rose
Row 16	Dusty Rose	Dusty Rose	Dusty Rose

Illustrations

Figure 1 diagrams all the key elements of the oval rug. You will refer to this illustration a number of times as you follow the instructions. In all the illustrations, black, white, and gray indicate different colors of wool.

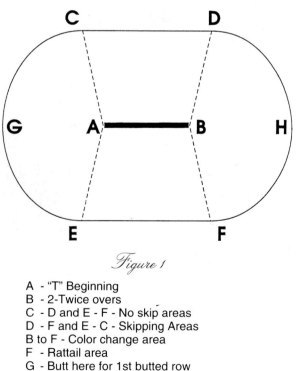

Figure 1

A - "T" Beginning
B - 2-Twice overs
C - D and E - F - No skip areas
D - F and E - C - Skipping Areas
B to F - Color change area
F - Rattail area
G - Butt here for 1st butted row
H - Butt here on last row

T-start

All braided rugs begin with a *T-start*.

1. Cut or rip one strand each of your chosen colors 1-1/2 inches (4 cm) wide. If the selvage is bulky, cut it off.

2. Put the right side of one strip facing up.

Tip Some wool looks alike on both sides. Other wool has a flat side, which I call the right side, and a fuzzy side, called the wrong side. Other braiders like to use the fuzzy side as the right side. Whichever you choose, be consistent. Always sew the right sides of the wool together.

1. Put the right side of a second strip at right angles on the end of the first strip (right side down). In other words, place the right sides together (figure 2).

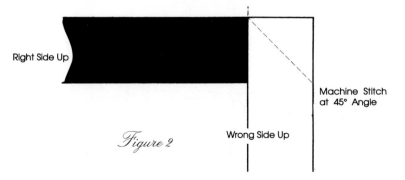

Right Side Up

Machine Stitch at 45° Angle

Figure 2

Wrong Side Up

2. Machine stitch from the top left corner to the side, using matching thread (figure 2). Trim close to the stitching, leaving approximately 1/8 inch (.5 cm) as shown in figure 3.

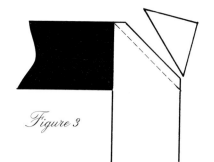

Figure 3

3. Working on the wrong side of the combined strips, turn in 1/4 inch (1 cm) on both sides of the diagonal seam for 2 to 3 inches (5 to 7.5 cm); pin to hold. Overcast both the top and bottom, using matching sewing thread (figure 4). The stitches should not show on the right side.

4. Take a third strip and fold the edges into the center. Fold again to the center and blind stitch the edge for 2 to 3 inches (5 to 7.5 cm), using matching thread (figure 5).

5. Sew this tube firmly to the center on the lower seam. Position the folded edges to the left (figure 6).

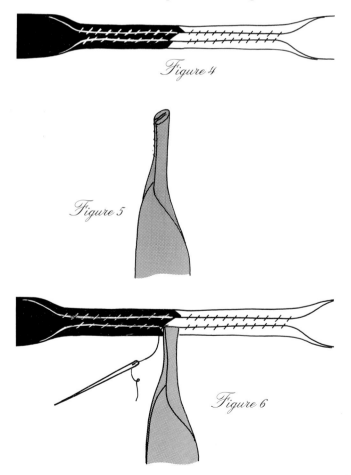

Figure 4

Figure 5

Figure 6

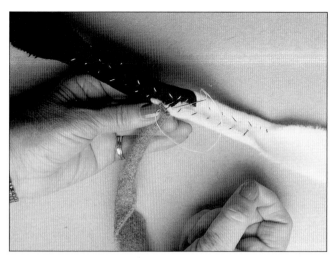

Attaching the third strip to the center

6. Fold the top half of the combined strips over the bottom half and blind stitch 2 to 3 inches (5 to 7.5 cm) on both sides of the center seam, enclosing the tube (figure 7). You have now completed the T.

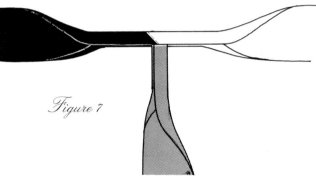

Figure 7

7. If you are using Braid-Aids, attach them to all three strips (see the photograph below).

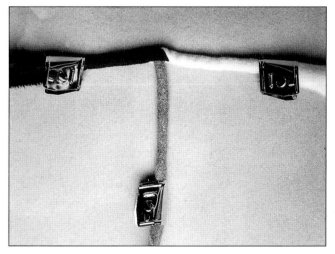

Braid-Aids in place on completed T

Braiding

1. Roll up one strand of wool to 2 feet (61.5 cm) from the *T* and pin. Keeping one strand shorter or rolled up throughout the braiding process keeps the three strands from tangling.

2. Hold the *T* so that the third tube has the fold on the left. Fold the edges in by hand or use Braid-Aids to fold.

3. Pull the right tube *over* the center tube and hold (figure 8). *Always keep the folds on the left.*

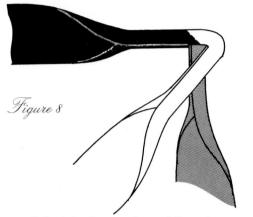

Figure 8

4. Now pull the left tube *over* the middle to the center and twist so the fold is on the left (figure 9). Hold with your left hand.

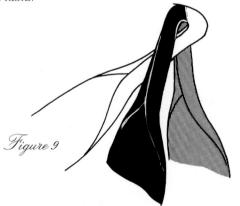

Figure 9

5. Continue braiding. Fold the edges in, take from the right, put the tube in the center and hold with the right hand. Now fold the edges in on the strand on the left, pull tightly to the center, and hold with the left hand. Make sure your folds are on the left. Check the other side of the braid to make sure that the folds aren't showing.

6. Put a large safety pin through the loops to hold the braid together when you stop.

7. Braid for 2 inches (5 cm) and put the braid into the clamp. Always keep some tension on your clamp. Pull as you're braiding (see photographs opposite).

8. Braid for 13 inches (33 cm), and then braid two *twice overs*.

   a. Take a tube on the right and braid (figure 10a).

   b. Take the next tube from the *right,* braid and hold (figure 10b).

   c. Braid the tube from the left and pull *tightly* (figure 10c).

   d. Repeat a, b, and c once more (figure 11).

This is the only time a corner is braided in.

9. Braid about 36 inches (92.5 cm). When you attach your strips, place the right sides together as per figure 2 and trim as in figure 3.

Tip You may want to take your braid out now and practice until you have an even, tight braid.

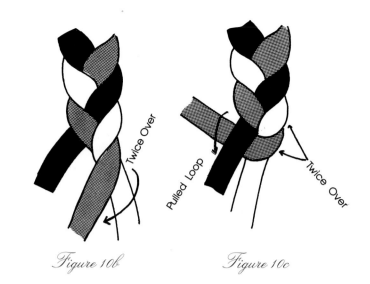

Figure 10a   *Figure 10b*   *Figure 10c*

Lacing

1. Now we're ready to *lace* or sew the braid together. Take about 5 feet (152.4 cm) of lacing thread. Thread it into the *tapestry* needle and knot.

Tip Keep the right side of the rug up; this is the side that is up when you are braiding.

2. Position the *T* away from you and to your left (figure 11).

3. Insert the needle through the wool *into* the second *pulled loop*. After braiding twice overs, the single loop on the opposite side is pulled tightly, therefore called a pulled loop. This attaches the thread firmly and hides the knot (figure 12).

4. The lacing technique for the first 13 inches (33 cm)—the first row—is different from the rest of the rug. The reason is that the braid in these first inches (until the *T* is reached) goes in the opposite direction from the braid in the next 13 inches (33 cm).

There are two methods of lacing this first 13 inches (33 cm).

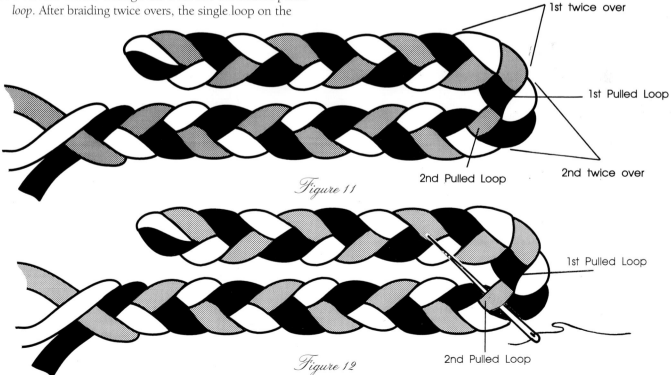

Figure 11

Figure 12

Figure 13

Figure 14

Figure 15

Figure 16

Method #1

Insert the tapestry needle as mentioned above and shown in figure 12. Sew each loop, alternating the sides on the fold side of the braid (figure 13). Pull the lacing thread tightly after each stitch. Continue until you reach the *T*.

This method is easy to do. The stitches are hidden, it is sewn tightly, and the loops are alternating as in the rest of the rug.

Method #2:

Method #2 is called a *reverse e* because the stitches look like an "e" going backward (figure 18). This method has been the accepted way for many years.

a. Insert the tapestry needle as in figure 12. Now switch to the *lacing needle* (the Braidkin).

b. Insert the lacing needle through the space between the next loop to the left (figure 14).

c. Cross to the upper braid, insert the needle into the opposite loop going from the left to right. Use the lacing needle to hide the thread and pull (figure 15).

d. Cross back down to the lower braid, lace in the loop already laced, going toward the left (figure 16).

e. Lace in the loop to its left (for the first time). Hide the thread and pull (figure 17). For example: Go from 1 to 2, then up to 3 (going from left to right), back to 4 again and then to 5 (figure 18).

This method is harder to learn. If you're using three strands of solid colored wool, it is a bit hard to hide your stitches. It also leaves a line down the center because your stitches aren't woven together, as in the rest of the rug.

It is a good idea to learn both methods as both have advantages.

The directions from here on are the same for both methods.

5. Lace until you reach the *T*.

6. Switch to the tapestry needle. Insert it through the bottom of the *T*, halfway from the bottom to the top. Take a 1/4-inch (1 cm) stitch. Skip one loop on the braid you are attaching and lace the next loop. Pull the thread. *Turn your rug* as you are going around the *T*.

7. Take a 1/4-inch (1 cm) stitch at the end of the *T* and skip the next loop on the row you are attaching; lace the next loop (figure 19).

8. Take one more stitch on the other side of the *T*, skip a loop on the row you're attaching (working braid), then lace the next loop.

The *T* is now laced.

9. Return the thread to the lacing needle.

10. The following is the technique to be used for the rest of the rug.

a. Lace only in one direction—toward your *left*.
b. Lace through the loop to the left of the *T*, going from right to left; pull the thread.
c. Lace the next loop in the braid you are attaching. Cross up to the body of rug and lace going from right to left. Hide the lacing thread and pull, *holding both braids flat as you pull* (figure 20).
d. Continue lacing in this manner until you reach the curved end. *Never skip on the straight side of the rug. Lace in every loop.*
e. Skip four times on this second curve (skip every other loop). *Skip only on the outside braid— never on the body of the rug.*

11. Continue braiding and lacing until three rows are completed.

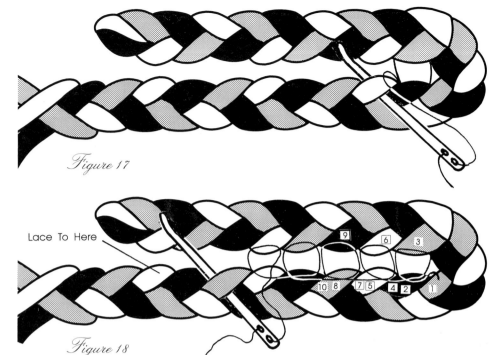

Figure 17

Figure 18

Lace To Here

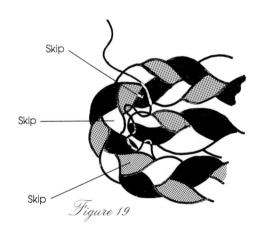

Skip

Skip

Skip

Figure 19

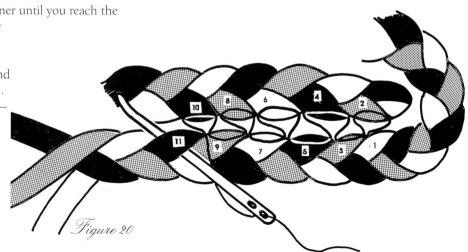

Figure 20

45

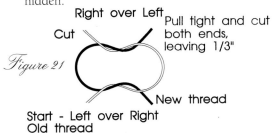

Tip To attach a new piece of lacing thread, use a square knot: Left over right and around; then right over left and around. Pull tightly (figure 21). Always hide the knot. Push it into the folds with the lacing needle and check the back of the rug to make sure it's completely hidden.

Right over Left

Cut

Pull tight and cut both ends, leaving 1/3"

Figure 21

New thread

Start - Left over Right
Old thread

General Rules for Lacing and Skipping

It's a good practice to braid a row and then lace it. This is the time to decide if you want to change a color. Here are some general rules for mastering lacing.

▼ Four to six skips (increases) on the curve normally will keep it flat. Space your skips evenly around the curve.

▼ Skip about the same number of times on both ends of the row.

▼ If the rug scallops, there are too many skips. If it cups up, there are not enough.

▼ Establish a routine; for example, lace three loops (on the braid you are attaching) and skip one loop all around the curve. The key is to skip evenly and alternate your skips. As the rug gets bigger, the skips get farther apart. Figure 22 diagrams the approximate placement of skips and shows where to change colors.

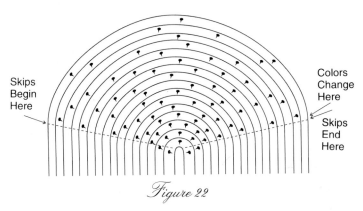

Skips Begin Here

Colors Change Here

Skips End Here

Figure 22

▼ It is impossible to make a hard and fast rule regarding how many skips and how often. If you have changed the width of your braid, skip less if it is wider; skip more if it is narrower.

Lacing and Skipping on the Oval Rug

▼ When lacing on the curved ends, always lace the loop on the braid you are attaching; then lace the next loop on the body of the rug. Hold flat and pull. Evaluate whether to skip the next loop on the row you are attaching. If the lacing thread is ahead of the next loop on the row you are attaching (working braid), skip it and lace the next loop. Now lace the top loop on the body of the rug (figure 23).

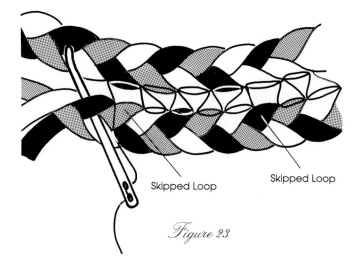

Skipped Loop

Skipped Loop

Figure 23

▼ Starting on the third row, put a T-pin in every skipped loop. Keep them in place for approximately five rows.

▼ Avoid skipping in the same place. If you place a pin where you skip, it will mark the place where you skipped in the previous rows.

▼ Mark the *T* and the twice overs with a large straight pin on A and B (figure 1). This will help you know when it is time to start thinking about starting or ending your skips.

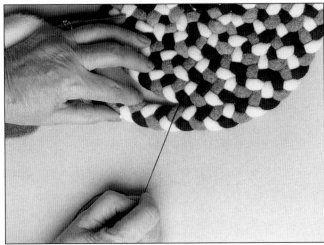

Not ready to skip

Time to skip

▼ Start skipping when the ends of the rug start forming the curve. Early or late skips will make barbells or bulges where it should be straight.

▼ Check the straight sides of your rug every row for these first two to four rows; line the side up with the edge of the table and mold the rug into a straight line. Your rug will be pliable now. If it is banana-shaped now, you won't be able to correct this later.

Tip The photographs below show regular lacing. Notice how I laced the plaid in the photograph on the left, pulling the braid open. This enables the thread to line up in the space between the loops so that the lacing thread can be hidden. The other photograph shows lacing the top loop. Hold the braids together and pull tightly to hide the lacing thread with the needle.

Changing Colors

When you change colors, you want to avoid being obvious; you want your new color to make its appearance in a subtle fashion. To change colors successfully, follow these steps:

1. Change to a new color on the opposite end of the *T* (figure 1 and figure 22).

2. Complete 3 rows (or the number of rows you would like before making a color change.)

3. Braid beyond the curve.

4. Hold a ruler along the straight side of the rug or put the rug along the side of a table.

5. The outside loop to the right of the edge is the loop to remove.

6. Put a T-pin *above* and *below* the preceding loop in the loop to be removed (figure 24).

Color To Be Removed

Figure 24

Lacing the braid you are attaching

Lacing the top loop

7. Unbraid 2 inches (5 cm) beyond the T-pins and cut between them at a 45-degree angle (figure 25).

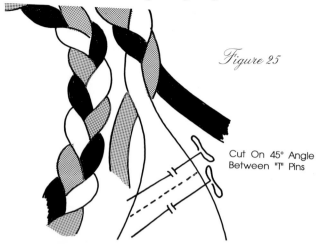

Figure 25

Cut On 45° Angle
Between "T" Pins

New color sewn on

Cutting between the T-pins

Braiding with new color

Placement of new color

Sewn edge concealed by braid

New color appears in braid

8. Sew the strip of new color to the unbraided strip you just cut; sew along the cut line. Rebraid the three strands. The seam you just sewed should be under the preceding loop; the new color will be on the right side of the braid.

9. Continue braiding, lacing, and changing colors as per the color chart on page 40 until you've completed 14 rows or the number of rows you need to almost finish the rug.

10. Change only one color at a time to blend colors well.

Tip Some braiders hide their seam when attaching a new strip. This is done by having the seam fall under the loop as shown in figures 24 and 25. I recommend hiding the seam if you're using solid colors as in the "Watermelon" rug (page 35) or "Country Spring" (page 39). If your rug is tweedy, or when you use more neutral or darker colors, the seams don't show anyway. I have never found that these seams wear quickly. Tight, sewing machine stitches hold up well. If you are attaching strips by hand, it may be better to hide the seam.

Rattailing or Tapering

Rattailing or tapering is a method of ending a continuous braid. Many braiders end their rugs this way. I use rattailing at the point in the rug where I want the continuous braid to end; then I butt to finish the rug.

1. Refer to figures 1 and 26 (above, right) for areas to rattail. Put a T-pin in the braid where the curve ends. This is where the braid should end.

2. Cut off the braid 1 inch (2.5 cm) below this pin and unbraid 8 inches (20.5 cm).

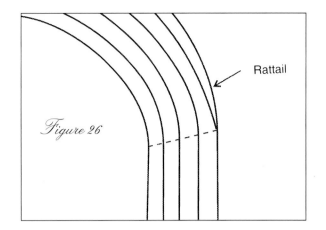

Figure 26

Rattail

3. To taper, cut all three strands so that they measure 5/8 inch (1.6 cm) on the ends; cut up both sides for 6–8 inches, gradually widening your cut until the wool is a normal width (photo below).

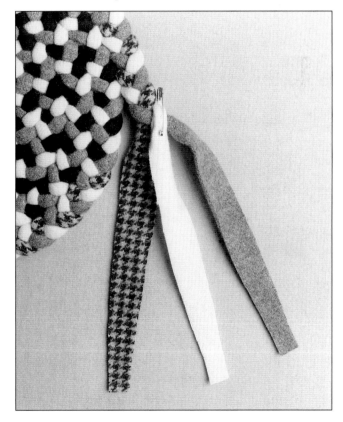

Strands cut to 5/8 inch (1.6 cm) on ends

4. Rebraid the rattail as far as you can, still folding the edges in. When the rattail gets so narrow that the edges can no longer be folded by hand, blind stitch the remaining edges. These ends should be as small as you can make them. Braid all but the final inch (2.5 cm) and pin to hold.

5. Lace to the last inch (2.5 cm).

Lacing the rattail to the last inch

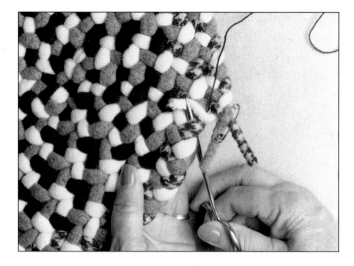

First strand ready to pull in

6. Using needle-nose pliers, weave the most obvious color strand into its matching color in the rug, if possible. Pull through one loop onto the body of the rug (figure 28). Twist the remaining two loops around each other and weave the next most obvious color through the next loop in the rug. Weave the final loop in the same color loop in the rug. If this doesn't look smooth or is too obvious, try again. Sometimes you can do better using a different combination.

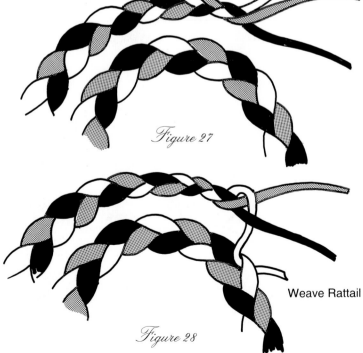

Figure 27

Weave Rattail

Figure 28

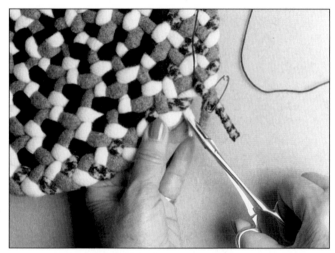

Pulling in first strand

Pulling in second strand

Pulling in third strand

7. Cut the ends of the loops (on the back of rug) even with the side of the loop it was pulled through. Take a needle and matching thread and sew to secure these ends. This completes your continuous braid.

Butting

Butting is a method of forming one complete row by weaving the two ends of a braid together to form a necklace; then you lace the necklace around the rug. All loose ends are carefully concealed. Butting seamlessly frames, and thereby finishes, the rug. I always end my rugs with one or two butted rows.

Butting is also the best technique for radically changing colors without showing a color change area; my "Americana" rug on page 70 is a good example of how that approach works.

In addition, butting protects the rattail from coming unraveled. And it is a wonderful way to add rows to large rugs and thereby avoid having to carry the whole rug to the sewing machine every time you need to add strands of wool to your continuous braid.

The last point I need to make here is that butting is the most challenging aspect of making a braided rug. In my classes, this is the technique students need the most help with. An easy way to visualize butting is to think of it as joining two ends of braid together by weaving same-colored loops through each other. Once you get the hang of it, you'll be able to butt with the best of them.

If you are butting the whole rug, or any part of it, use the following directions.

Butting - Row 15 (or your next to the last row)

1. Fold in the edges of all three strands. Pin each strand with a #2 (large) safety pin (figure 29).

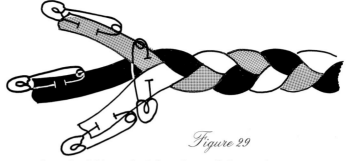

Figure 29

2. Place the folds to the left and put all three tubes into your clamp. The large pins will hold the tubes in the clamp.

Three tubes secured in clamp

3. Braid a few inches (5 or 6 cm) and put a fourth pin across all the loops (figure 29).

4. Braid until you have a length of braid long enough to go around the rug once.

Length of braid ready to butt

5. Place the ends to be butted on a curve (figure 1). Remember to place the braid clockwise (in the same direction as the rest of the rug), with the top of your braid up.

6. Leave 5-6 inches (13-15 cm) of lacing thread and start lacing 4 inches (10 cm) from the beginning of the braid.

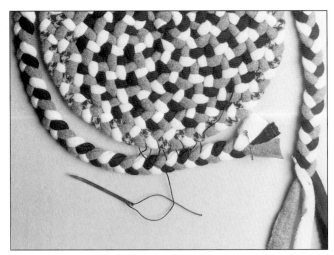

Beginning of lacing butted rug

7. Lace all around the rug, leaving 4 inches (10 cm) unlaced on the end.

8. Braid enough so that you can overlap the two ends of your braid by 3-4 inches (7.5-10 cm).

9. Place the pinned end of the braid (the beginning) on top of the other end. Match the same colors: for example, place white on top of white, gray on top of gray (figure 30).

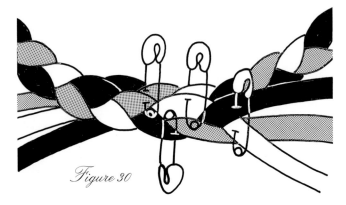

Figure 30

Tip Double-check to be sure the braid is long enough; you need to have enough braid to lace the final 8 inches (20.5 cm) to the rug without stretching the braid.

10. Pin two matching loops together on the fold side (inside); for example, pin white to white, and gray to gray. Pin the third loops (between these two) together on the outside (figure 30).

Beginning of row pinned over end of row

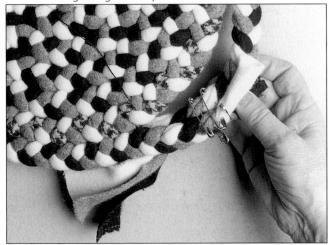

Matching colors pinned together

11. Take out any pins left on the ends and unbraid to the pinned loops. Cut the ends of the braid so that approximately 2 inches (5 cm) remain on each end of the braid.

Cutting off extra wool

12. You will start to butt with the ends of one loop of each color free on the fold side. Both loops will be free on the outside (figure 31).

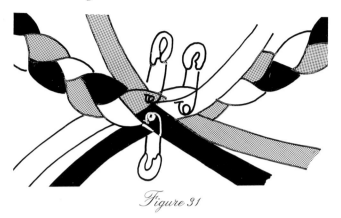

Tip Hold onto the butting area firmly with your left hand; don't let go. Do all of your pinning, etc., with your right hand.

Removing pins; hold firmly in left hand

13. Work with the outside loops. Cross the top loop over the bottom loop and pull out all the fullness. Make sure the edges are folded in. Unpin and repin along the side of the braid (figure 32).

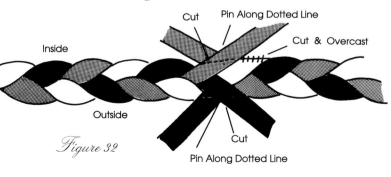

Cut
Pin Along Dotted Line

Inside

Cut & Overcast

Outside

Figure 32

Cut
Pin Along Dotted Line

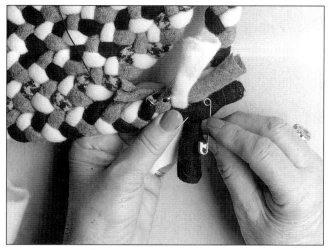

Repinning along edge

14. Next work on the loop to the right on the fold side. Insert the lacing needle in front of the back loop and pull the end up and out; it will be crossed behind its matching loop. Pull to tighten. Unpin and repin along the edge of the braid.

Pulling inside loop through and crossing over

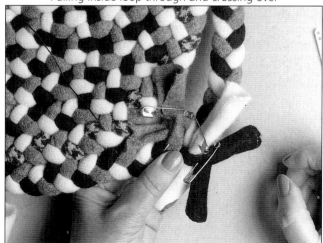

Pinning lengthwise

53

15. Using the lacing needle, insert it in front of the front loop on the left. Pull the end out; it will cross in front of the matching loop. Pull out all the fullness. Unpin and repin along the edge of the braid. You have now woven your two ends together.

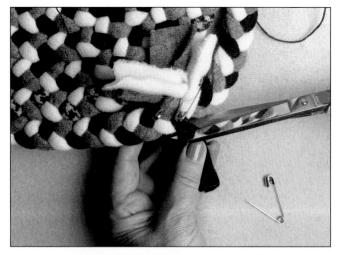

Cutting outside loop even with edge of rug

Pulling last loop through

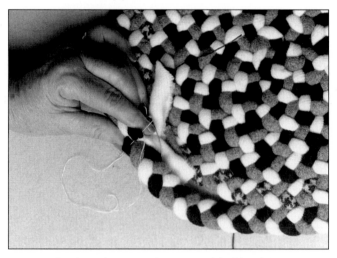

Sewing edges together even with side of rug

Crossing over and pinning lengthwise

16. Unpin the outside loops and cut both the front and back loops even with the edge of the braid (figure 32). Hold the cut edges together. Overcast firmly with matching thread.

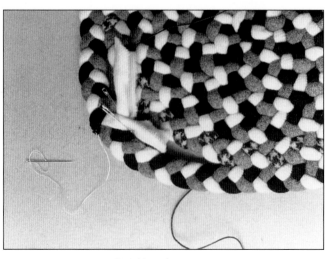

Outside edge, sewn

17. Repeat for the top loops. Cut the loops on the right even with the edge of the braid and overcast. Then cut the loops on the left even with the braid and overcast. The sewn edges should fall between the rows so the stitching doesn't show.

18. Lace the final 8 inches (20.5 cm) of braid to the rug. Weave the lacing thread through the loops until you come back to where you started to lace and tie.

All loops cut and sewn

Butting - Last Row

The instructions for the last row are a bit different—all your butting seams are on the fold side (inside). Repeat steps 1-9. Then continue with steps 19-28.

19. Pin all three loops on the inside, with one pin on the outside, just to hold (figure 33).

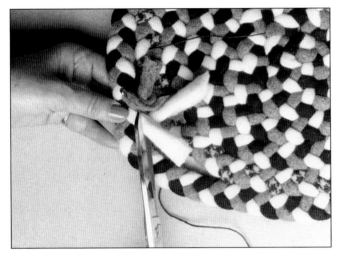
Cutting next loop even with edge

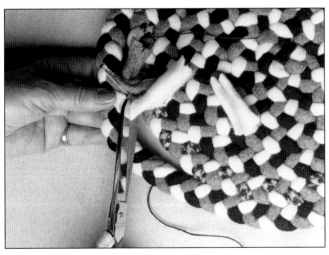
Cutting second loop even with edge

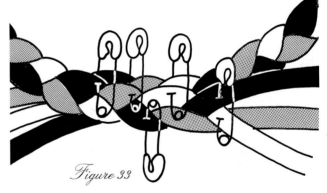
Figure 33

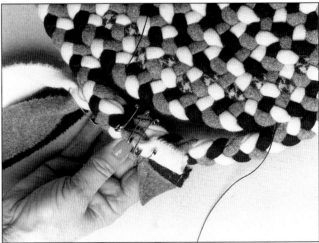
Pinning matching colors

20. Unbraid to the pinned loops. Take out any pins left on the ends. Cut the end of the braid so that only about 2 inches (5 cm) remains on the end of the braid.

Extra braid cut off

21. You will be starting to butt with only two strands in the final place (up), one on the left, and one on the right (figure 34). Hold firmly and remove the outside pin.

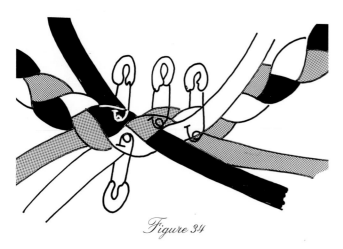

Figure 34

22. Insert the lacing needle into the front of the middle loop and pull the end up and out. Insert the needle into the front of the rear middle loop. Pull the loop up and out. Cross the front over the back, pull out any fullness, making sure the edges are turned in. Unpin and repin evenly with the side of the braid.

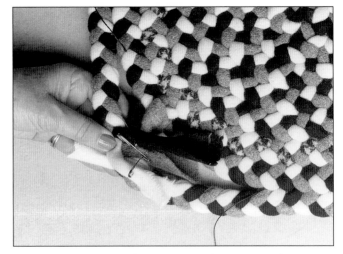

Third loop after first and second loops are pulled through and pinned

23. Work on the loop to the left. Insert the needle into the front loop, pull it out, cross over the back loop, pull out the fullness, and pin. Unpin and repin evenly with the side of the braid (figure 35).

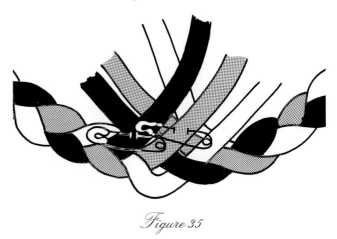

Figure 35

24. Unpin the right loop. Pull the inside loop out of the braid, *slip your finger in where the loop came out, and insert the outside loop in the hole, pulling it toward the fold side.* Pull the fullness out, fold the edges in, cross over the back loop, and pin (figure 35). The last row is now woven together.

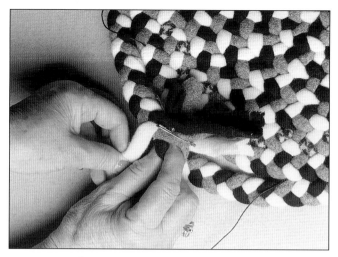

Putting fingers through braid where loop came out

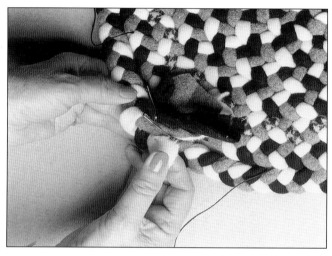

Inserting outside loop through hole

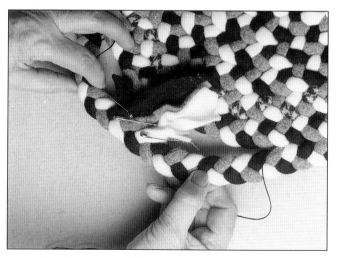

Crossing over and pinning even with outside edge

25. Unpin the loops to the right, cut evenly along the edge, and overcast firmly with matching thread.

26. Repeat with the middle and left side loops. All of the seams should fall between the rows so the joined ends don't show (figure 36).

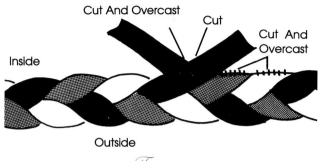

Figure 36

27. Lace the final 8 inches (20.5 cm) to the rug.

28. Weave the ends of the lacing thread through the loops until they meet, and tie.

Congratulations! You have just completed your oval braided rug. I'm sure you now have your own stories about this "first rug" to share with friends and family.

The Circle Braided Rug

▼ ▼ ▼

$\mathcal{T}$he circle is also an easy rug for the beginner. If your braid isn't even, you can accommodate the difference by spacing your skips closer or farther apart. If your braid widens, you can skip less often. If your braid narrows, you can skip more frequently. Of course, if you maintain a braid of consistent width, you will wind up with a smoother and more uniform rug.

A circle lends itself well to either a shaded rug or a hit-or-miss style. If you are shading, change one color at a time in various places all around the circle—not in one spot, as in the oval. If you are shading lighter, remove the darkest strand; if you are shading darker, remove the lightest strand.

Materials

Bluebell is a circle, 4 feet, 5 inches (1.2 m, 13 cm) wide. You will need about 11 pounds (5 kilos) of wool. It is a monochromatic rug in shades of blue and gray. Review the list of equipment you'll need on page 36. Make sure you have matching sewing thread.

Starting the Circle

1. *T-start* as in the oval directions, following steps 1-7 on pages 40–41.

2. Attach Braid-Aids, if you are using them.

Color Plan

Rows 1-5	Med. Blue Tweed	Med. Blue Tweed	Lt. Gray Tweed
Row 6	Darker Blue Tweed	Med. Blue Tweed	Blue/White Check
Rows 7 & 8	Med. Blue Tweed	Med. Blue Tweed	Blue/White Check
Row 9	Dark Blue	Med. Blue Tweed	Blue/White Check
Rows 10-12	Dark Blue	Dark Blue Tweed	Blue/White Check
Rows 13 & 14	Med. Blue	Dark Blue Tweed	Blue/White Check
Rows 15 & 16	Med. Blue	Dark Blue Tweed	Lt. Gray Tweed
Rows 17 & 18	Med. Blue	Lt. Gray Tweed	Lt. Gray Tweed
Rows 19-21	Wedgewood Blue	Lt. Gray Tweed	Lt. Gray Tweed
Row 22	Wedgewood Blue	Lt. Gray Tweed	Lt. Blue
Rows 23 & 24	Lt. Blue Tweed	Lt. Gray Tweed	Lt. Blue
Row 25	Lt. Blue Tweed	Med. Gray Tweed	Lt. Blue
Row 26	Blue & White Tweed	Med. Gray Tweed	Blue & White Tweed
Rows 27 & 28	Blue & White Tweed	Med. Gray Tweed	Med. Blue
Row 29	Blue & White Tweed	Med. Gray Tweed	Darker Blue
Row 30	Darker Blue & White Tweed	Med. Gray Tweed	Darker Blue
Row 31	Darker Blue & White Tweed	Darker Blue Tweed	Darker Blue
Rows 32-35	Dark Blue Tweed	Darker Blue Tweed	Darker Blue

3. Roll up one strand to 2 feet (61.5 cm) from the braid and pin to keep the strands from tangling.

4. Braid six twice overs as follows:

    a. Hold the *T* so the center tube has the fold on the left (figure 7, page 41).

    b. Pull the right tube over the center, keeping the fold on the left, and hold (figure 37a).

    c. Again, pull the tube on the right to the center, keeping the fold on the left (figure 37b).

    d. Pull the tube on the left to the center—pull tightly—and hold (leave the fold on the right). This one is called the pulled loop (figure 37c).

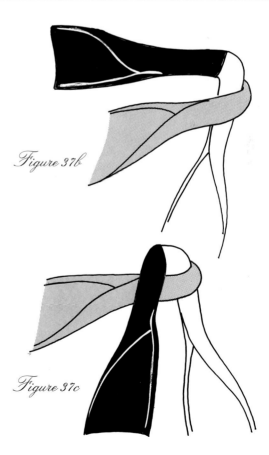

Figure 37b

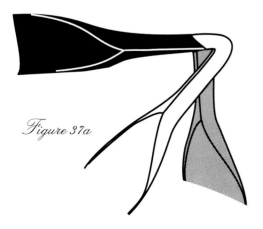

Figure 37a

Figure 37c

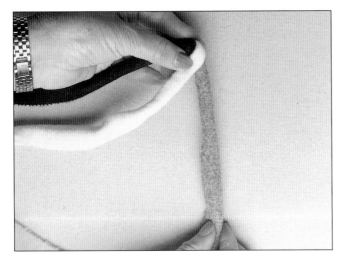

Pulling from right

Pulling from right again

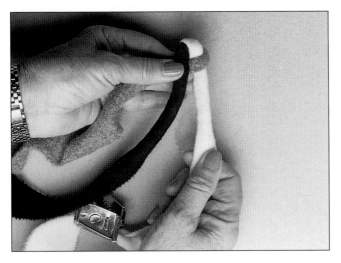

Pulling from left

5. Repeat steps a–c five more times (figures 38a, b, and c).

Figure 38a

Figure 38b

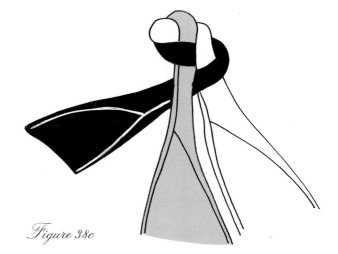

Figure 38c

6. On the third twice over, flat fold to the left the tube with the fold on the right, so that all the folds will be on the left. The center should have the curve braided in (figure 39).

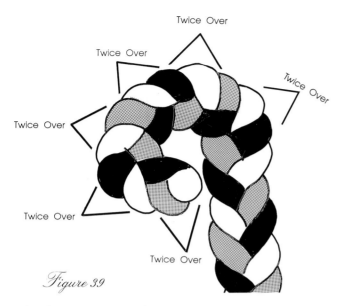

Twice Over
Twice Over
Twice Over
Twice Over
Twice Over
Twice Over

Figure 39

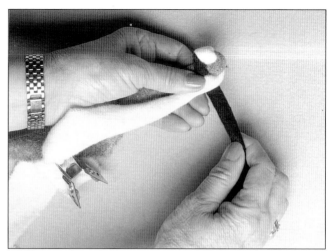

Pulling from right

7. After the six twice overs have been braided, put the braid into the clamp and braid normally for a the rest of the rug; that is, fold the edges in, pull from the right to the center and hold, then pull from the left to the center and hold, alternating from right to left (figures 8 and 9, page 42). When you stop, put a large safety pin through the loops. Figure 40 indicates all the key locations for making your circle.

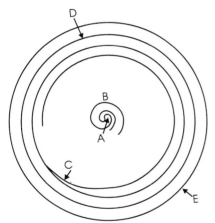

A - "T" Beginning
B - 6 Twice Overs
C - Rattail Area - 3rd To The Last Row
D - Butting Area - Next To The Last Row
E - Butting Area - Last Row

Figure 40

Pulling from right again

Lacing

1. Always lace on a flat surface. Take about 4 feet (1.2 m) of lacing thread, thread it into the tapestry needle, and knot.

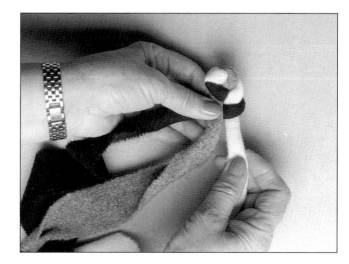

Pulling from left

2. Make sure the right side of the rug is facing you, with the T positioned away from you, and to your left (figure 41a). Form the braid into a circle and hold together tightly. Insert the needle into the third pulled loop—through the wool—to attach the thread and hide it (figure 41a).

3. Insert the needle into the T, and take a 1/4-inch (1 cm) stitch half way between the bottom and the top (figure 41b). Pull. Lace the fourth loop, using the blunt end of the tapestry needle; pull (figure 41c).

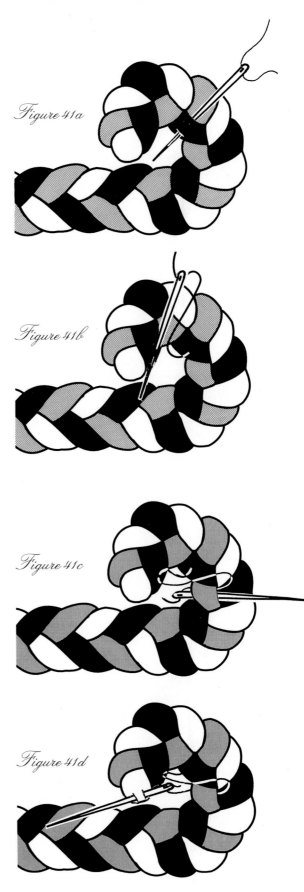

Figure 41a

Figure 41b

Figure 41c

Figure 41d

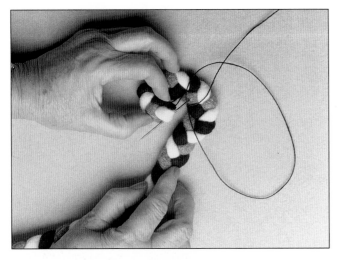

Lacing the T

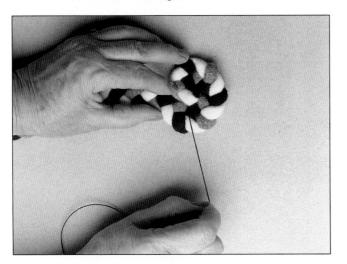

Pulling the stitch tightly at end of T

4. Take another 1/4-inch (1 cm) stitch into the end of the T (figure 41d), pull tightly, and switch to a lacing needle. The center of the circle should be closed tightly and the stitches hidden. The T is now laced.

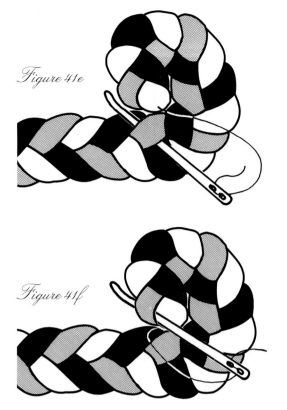

Figure 41e

Figure 41f

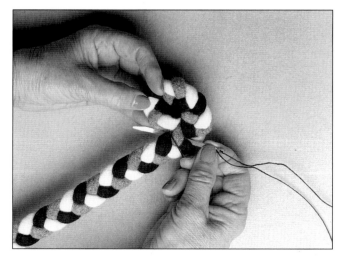

Lacing from the outside to the center

5. Continue lacing—going between the loops. Lace from the braid you are attaching to the body of the rug (figures 41e and 41f).

6. *Lace in every loop in the body of the rug. Skip only on the row you are attaching.* The skips will get farther apart as the circle gets bigger. For example, on row 1, lace one loop and skip one loop all the way around. On row 2, lace two and skip one—all the way around.

Tip Try to skip evenly around the rug; for example, if you are lacing five loops and skipping one, do it all the way around. Lace the row you are attaching, then lace the body of the rug; hold both braids flat, pull the lacing thread, and decide if you need to skip (figure 23, page 46).

7. Starting on row 4, put a T-pin in the skipped loop. Keep the pins in for four to five rows. Avoid skipping in the same place; alternate your skips (figure 22, page 46).

More Tips About Lacing and Skipping

▼ If the rug scallops, you are skipping too often. On the next row, try not to skip at all. This will take out the fullness. Then resume a normal pattern of skips.

▼ If the rug buckles in the center, you are not skipping enough. You need to take out your lacing until the rug is flat; then resume lacing, making sure to skip more often.

▼ A well-shaped circle is accomplished by skipping loops evenly and alternating your skips on the row you're attaching.

Changing Colors

Vary the place where you make your color changes. New colors should appear on the outside loop (figures 24 and 25, page 47 and page 48).

Rattailing

The method of rattailing is the same as for the oval rug directions except that you can rattail anywhere in your circle (see steps 3-7, figures 27 and 28, page 50. The larger the circle, the longer the rattail should be. For a chair pad, taper a 6-inch (15 cm) strip to an 8-inch (20.5 cm) strip. For larger circles, taper a 10-inch (25.5 cm) strip to a 20-inch (51 cm) strip.

Butting

Follow the oval rug directions for butting on page 51.

The Heart Braided Rug

▼ ▼ ▼

The heart is one of the most admired braided rugs. However, this shape is not for the beginner. It is best to make a few oval or circles first to learn to braid evenly, skip well, and practice doing twice overs. The heart requires practice; to ensure a well-balanced heart, you need to stop braiding at both the top and bottom v, and lace up to that point, so that you can braid the twice over in just the right spot.

Materials

"Country Heart" is 31 by 41 inches (79.5 x 105 cm) and requires about 4-1/2 pounds (2.1 kilos) of wool. Review the equipment list on page 36. Purchase matching sewing thread.

T-start

T-start as per the oval directions, steps 1-7, page 40 and page 41, then braid straight for 11 inches (28 cm) as per steps 1-7, page 42. Figure 42 diagrams all the key elements of the heart-shaped rug.

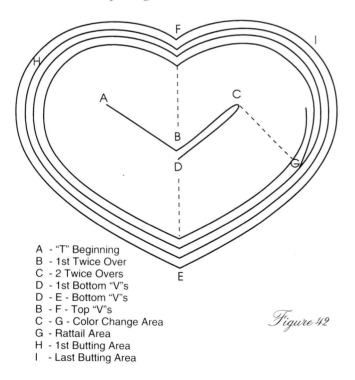

A - "T" Beginning
B - 1st Twice Over
C - 2 Twice Overs
D - 1st Bottom "V"s
D - E - Bottom "V"s
B - F - Top "V"s
C - G - Color Change Area
G - Rattail Area
H - 1st Butting Area
I - Last Butting Area

Figure 42

Twice overs

1. Braid one twice over.
   a. Take the tube on the left and braid (figure 43a).
   b. Take the tube from the *left* again and braid (figure 43b).
   c. Braid the tube from the *right* and pull tightly (figure 43c). The first center v is now braided in.

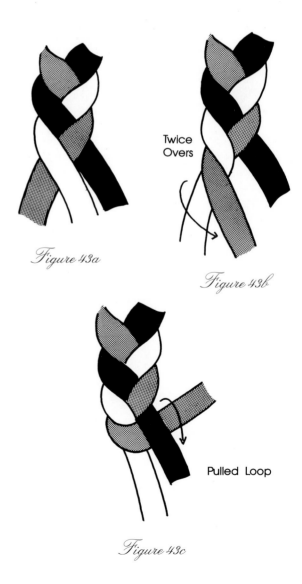

Twice Overs

Figure 43a

Figure 43b

Pulled Loop

Figure 43c

Color Plan

Rows 1-4	Dusty Rose	Mauve	Pink & Gray Check
Row 5	Plum	Mauve	Pink & Gray Check
Row 6	Plum	Maroon	Pink & Gray Check
Row 7	Plum	Maroon	Dark Blue Green
Row 8	Dark Blue	Maroon	Dark Blue Green
Row 9	Dark Blue	Medium Blue	Dark Blue Green
Row 10	Dark Turquoise	Medium Blue	Dark Blue Green
Row 11	Dark Turquoise	Medium Blue	Lt Blue & White Check
Row 12	Dusty Rose	Medium Blue	Lt Blue & White Check
Row 13	Dusty Rose	Light Pink	Pink & Gray Check
Row 14	Dusty Rose	Plum	Dark Pink & Gray Check
Row 15	Maroon	Plum	Dark Pink & Gray Check

2. Braid 11 inches (28 cm) more; then braid two twice overs, this time turning in the opposite direction.

    a. Take the tube on the right and braid (figure 44a).

    b. Take the next tube from the *right*, braid and hold (figure 44b).

    c. Braid the tube from the *left* and pull tightly (figure 44c).

    d. Repeat steps 2a, b, and c once more. This is the only time two twice overs are braided in (figures 11, page 43, and figure 42).

Figure 44a

Figure 44b

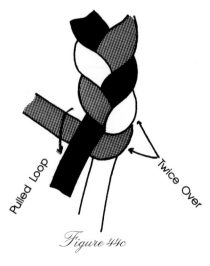

Figure 44c

Braiding

Braid another 11 inches (28 cm) and begin to lace.

Lacing

Lace the first 11 inches (28 cm) using either the reverse e method or the sewing method as shown in figures 12-18. Lace until the center *v* is reached.

Braiding and Lacing First V

1. Braid a single corner as in figures 44a, b, and c. Braid this corner so that the pulled loop on the row you are attaching falls *between* the twice over loops on row 1.

2. Lace as per figure 45.

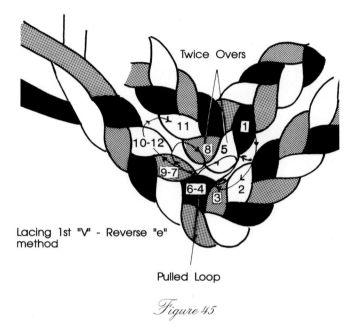

Lacing 1st "V" - Reverse "e" method

Figure 45

3. Continue lacing in reverse e method or sewing method until you reach the *T*.

4. Switch to a tapestry needle and sew the *T* as per the oval direction, steps 6-8, figure 19. Return the thread to your lacing needle and lace the rest of the heart in the regular way, going into every loop until the top *v* is reached.

Braiding and Lacing Top and Bottom Vs

1. Braid the top *v* as you did in figures 43a, b, and c, braiding twice from the left, then braiding a pulled loop from the right.

2. Braid the twice overs so that when lacing, you lace the twice overs, then skip the pulled loop on the body of the rug (figure 46).

3. Continue braiding and lacing until the curved end is reached. Lace this as you did the oval rug (page 46).

4. Continue braiding and lacing until you reach the bottom *v*.

5. Braid in a twice over as per figures 44a, b, and c. Braid the twice over so that the pulled loop on the braid you are attaching falls after the twice-over loops on the body of the rug.

6. Lace the twice-over loops, then skip the pulled loop.

7. Continue braiding, lacing, and braiding in *vs* until four rows are finished. Change one color as per color plan. Refer to figure 42 for color change area.

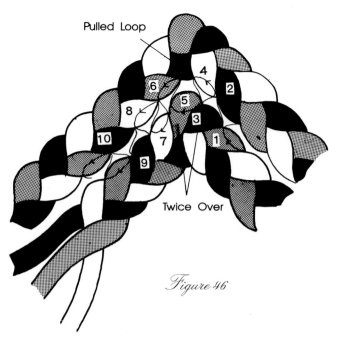

Pulled Loop

Twice Over

Figure 46

Continuing the Rug

Continue braiding, lacing, and changing colors as per the color chart until you have completed 13 rows.

Rattailing or Tapering

Rattailing is the same as in the oval; refer to figure 42 for the rattail area.

Butting

Rows 14 and 15 are the same as for the oval and circle; see figure 42 for the butting area.

General Rules for Lacing and Skipping

These rules are the same for the heart as for the oval and circle, with one exception: try to force skips farther around the curve toward both the top and bottom vs. This fills out the heart shape.

Tip Don't skip so much that the rug scallops (figure 47).

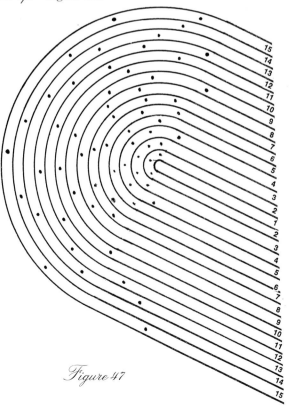

Figure 47

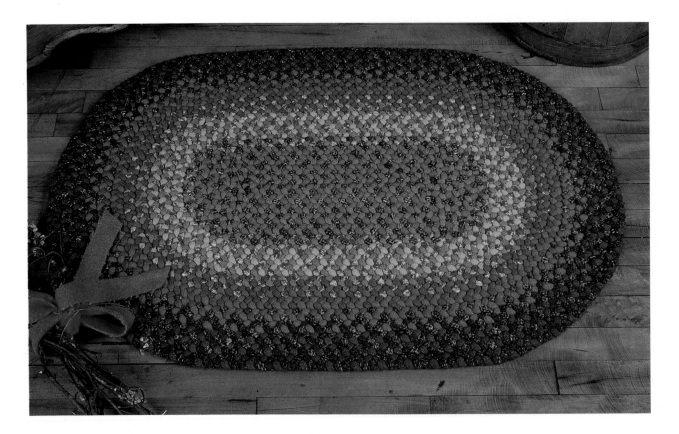

Bittersweet
2'3" x 3'3" (69 x 100 cm)

Color Plan

Rows 1-5	Orange	Camel	Dk. Brown Tweed
Row 6	Orange Plaid	Camel	Dk. Brown Tweed
Rows 7-9	Orange Plaid	Camel	Lt. Tan
Row 10	Orange Plaid	Camel	Med. Rust
Row 11	Orange Plaid	Taupe	Med. Rust
Row 12	Orange	Taupe	Med. Rust
Row 13	Orange	Taupe	Dk. Brown Tweed
Row 14	Orange	Dk. Brown Tweed	Dk. Brown Tweed
Rows 15-17	Dk. Rust	Dk. Brown Tweed	Dk. Brown Tweed

Amish
45" x 57" (115.5 x 146.5 cm)

Color Plan

Rows 1-5	Taupe	Mauve	Mauve & Black Plaid
Rows 6 & 7	Dusty Rose	Mauve	Mauve & Black Plaid
Rows 8 & 9	Lt. Dusty Rose	Mauve	Magenta (rattail)
Row 10	Lt. Dusty Rose	Black	Magenta
Row 11	Black	Black	Magenta
Row 12	Black	Royal Blue	Magenta
Rows 13 & 14	Wedgewood Blue	Royal Blue	Magenta
Row 15	Wedgewood Blue	Royal Blue	Wedgewood Blue
Row 16	Wedgewood Blue	Dk. Turquoise	Wedgewood Blue
Row 17	Wedgewood Blue	Dk. Turquoise	Med. Turquoise
Rows 18 & 19	Silver Gray	Dk. Turquoise	Med. Turquoise
Row 20	Silver Gray	Silver Gray	Med. Turquoise
Row 21	Silver Gray	Dusty Rose	Dk. Turquoise
Row 22	Magenta	Dusty Rose	Dk. Turquoise
Row 23	Magenta	Lt. Dusty Rose	Mauve
Row 24	Magenta	Med. Mauve	Mauve
Row 25	Magenta	Black	Mauve
Row 26	Magenta	Black	Mauve & Black Plaid
Row 27	Black	Black	Maroon
Row 28	Black	Black	Black

Americana
30" x 42" (77 x 108 cm)

Color Plan

Rows 1-7	Red	Gray	Blue/Red Plaid (rattail)
Row 8	Red	Red	Blue/Red Plaid
Row 9	Red	Red	Red
Row 10	Red	Navy	Blue/Red Plaid
Row 11	Navy	Navy	Blue/Red Plaid
Row 12	Navy	Navy	Navy
Rows 13-15	Navy	Gray	Blue/Red Plaid
Row 16	Navy	Red	Blue/Red Plaid
Row 17	Navy	Red	Red
Row 18	Red	Red	Red
Row 19	Navy	Navy	Navy

Country Spring Heart
30" x 40" (77 x 103 cm)

Color Plan

Rows 1-3	White	Med. Blue	Lt. Blue
Row 4	Lt. Pink	Med. Blue	Lt. Blue
Row 5	Lt. Pink	Med. Blue	Blue Gray Tweed
Row 6	Dusty Rose	Med. Blue	Blue Gray Tweed
Row 7	Dusty Rose	Med. Purple	Blue Gray Tweed
Row 8	Dusty Rose	Med. Purple	White
Row 9	Lt. Pink	Med. Purple	White
Row 10	Lt. Pink	Lt. Yellow	White
Row 11	Lt. Pink	Lt. Blue	White
Row 12	Med. Blue	Lt. Blue	White
Row 13	Med. Blue	Lt. Blue	Med. Green
Row 14	Med. Blue	Dusty Rose	Dusty Rose
Row 15	Dusty Rose	Dusty Rose	Dusty Rose

Western
3' x 5' (92.5 x 152.4 cm)

Color Plan

Rows 1-5	Lt. Tan	Lt. Rust	Lt. Tan Herringbone
Rows 6	Lt. Tan	Lt. Rust	Camel
Rows 7 & 8	Brown/Rust Plaid	Lt. Rust	Camel
Row 9	Brown/Rust Plaid	Taupe	Camel
Row 10	Brown/Rust Plaid	Taupe	Taupe
Row 11	Black	Taupe	Taupe
Row 12	Brown Herringbone	Taupe	Taupe
Row 13	Brown Herringbone	Taupe	Camel
Row 14	Brown Herringbone	Beige	Camel
Rows 15-17	Rust Herringbone	Beige	Camel
Row 18	Rust Herringbone	Rust Herringbone	Camel
Row 19	Rust Herringbone	Brown/Beige Check	Camel
Row 20	Rust	Brown/Beige Check	Camel
Row 21	Rust	Brown/Beige Check	Dk. Brown
Row 22	Rust	Dk. Brown	Dk. Brown
Row 23	Black	Dk. Brown	Dk. Brown

Kaleidoscope
45" x 45" (115.5 x 115.5 cm)

Color Plan

Rows 1-8	Med. Blue	Magenta	Blue Speckled
Rows 9-11	Med. Blue	Dark Purple	Blue Speckled
Rows 12 & 13	Med. Turquoise	Dark Purple	Blue Speckled
Row 14	Med. Turquoise	Lt. Turquoise	Blue Speckled
Rows 15 & 16	Med. Turquoise	Lt. Turquoise	Blue Gray Tweed
Rows 17 & 18	Med. Turquoise	Wedgewood Blue	Blue Gray Tweed
Rows 19-21	Bright Blue	Wedgewood Blue	Blue Gray Tweed
Row 22	Magenta	Wedgewood Blue	Blue Gray Tweed
Rows 23 & 24	Magenta	Wedgewood Blue	Blue Speckled
Rows 25-27	Magenta	Dk. Blue & Black Plaid	Purple
Rows 28-30	Royal Blue	Dk. Blue & Black Plaid	Purple

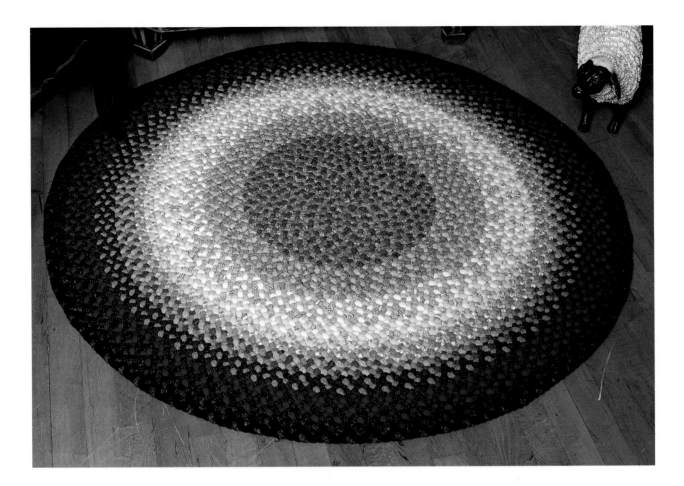

Coals On The Hearth
4' circle (123 cm)

Color Plan

Rows 1-10	Med. Gray/Red Plaid	Med. Gray	B&W Check
Rows 11-13	Light Gray	Med. Gray	B&W Check
Row 14	Light Gray	Med. Gray	Lighter B&W Check
Rows 15 & 16	Light Gray	White	Lighter B&W Check
Rows 17-19	Light Gray	White	Silver Gray
Row 20	Light Gray	Gray & White Check	Silver Gray
Row 21	Med. Gray	Gray & White Check	Med. Gray
Rows 22 & 23	Med. Gray	Med. Gray/Red Plaid	Dk. Gray
Rows 24-25	Med. Gray	B&R Check	Dk. Gray
Row 26	Old Red	B&R Check	Dk. Gray
Rows 27 & 28	Old Red	B&R Check	Black Plaid
Row 29	Black	B&R Check	Black Plaid
Row 30	Black	Black	Black Plaid

Victorian
4'9" scalloped (146 cm)

Color Plan

Rows 1-10	Lt. Beige Tweed	Lt. Taupe	Med. Taupe
Rows 11-13	Lt. Beige Tweed	Med. Taupe	Med. Taupe
Rows 14-16	Med. Taupe Tweed	Med. Taupe	Med. Taupe
Row 17	Med. Taupe Tweed	Med. Taupe	Black
Row 18	Blue Tweed	Med. Taupe	Black
Rows 19-20	Blue Tweed	Blue Plaid	Black
On Row 20, make six 6-inch braids an equal distance apart			
Row 21	Blue Plaid	Blue Plaid	Black
Row 22	Blue Plaid	Blue Plaid	Taupe
Row 23	Blue Plaid	Dusty Rose Tweed	Taupe
Row 24	Dusty Rose	Dusty Rose Tweed	Taupe
Row 25	Dusty Rose	Dusty Rose Tweed	Lt. Taupe Tweed
Row 26	Dusty Rose	Lt. Taupe	Lt. Taupe Tweed
Rows 27 & 28	Pink	Lt. Taupe	Lt. Taupe Tweed
Row 29	Pink	Lt. Taupe Tweed	Lt. Taupe Tweed
Row 30	Lt. Taupe Tweed	Lt. Taupe Tweed	Lt. Taupe Tweed

Nursery
5' x 7' (1.5 x 2.2 m)

Color Plan

Rows 1-5	Lt. Blue	Lt. Blue & White Plaid	Silver Gray
Row 6	Lt. Blue	Lt. Blue & White Plaid	Med. Gray
Row 7	Med. Blue	Lt. Blue & White Plaid	Med. Gray
Row 8	Med. Blue	Lt. Blue & White Plaid	Taupe
Row 9	Med. Blue	Med. Blue & White Plaid	Taupe
Rows 10 & 11	Dusty Rose	Med. Blue & White Plaid	Taupe
Row 12	Dusty Rose	Med. Taupe	Taupe
Row 13	Golden Brown	Med. Taupe	Taupe
Row 14	Golden Brown	Med. Taupe	Lt. Gray
Row 15	Golden Brown	Med. Gray	Lt. Gray
Row 16	Silver Gray	Med. Gray	Lt. Gray
Row 17	Lt. Green Plaid	Med. Gray	Lt. Gray
Row 18	Lt. Green Plaid	Med. Gray	Lt. Green
Row 19	Lt. Green Plaid	Lt. Yellow	Lt. Green
Rows 20 & 21	Lt. Yellow Green	Lt. Yellow	Lt. Green
Row 22	Lt. Yellow Green	Green & Yellow Plaid	Lt. Green
Row 23	Med. Green	Green & Yellow Plaid	Lt. Green
Row 24	Med. Green	Blue/Green Plaid	Lt. Green
Row 25	Med. Green	Blue/Green Plaid	Dk. Blue/Green Plaid
Row 26	Med. Green	Med. Blue Plaid	Dk. Blue/Green Plaid
Rows 27 & 28	Med. Blue	Med. Blue Plaid	Dk. Blue/Green Plaid
Row 29	Med. Blue	Med. Blue Plaid	Dk. Blue
Row 30	Med. Blue	Med. Blue Plaid	Taupe
Row 31	Med. Blue	Navy & White Tweed	Taupe
Row 32	Lt. Blue	Navy & White Tweed	Taupe
Row 33	Lt. Blue	Navy & White Tweed	Silver Gray
Row 34	Lt. Blue	Navy & White Tweed	Med. Blue Plaid
Row 35	Med. Blue	Navy & White Tweed	Med. Blue Plaid
Row 36	Dk. Blue	Dk. Blue	Navy Plaid

Bits and Pieces
60" circle (152 cm)

A hit-or-miss rug using scraps of brown, taupe, camel, beige, and plaids.

Nantucket
34" x 58" (87 x 149 cm)

Color Plan

Rows 1-5	Med. Blue	Gray	Blue Green Check
Rows 6-7	Med. Blue	Gray	Blue/White Check
Row 8	Med. Blue	Gray	Lt. Gray
Row 9	Lt. Green	Gray	Lt. Gray
Row 10	Lt. Green	Lt. Green	Lt. Gray
Row 11	Lt. Green	Lt. Green	Gray Check
Row 12	Lt. Green	Blue Green	Gray Check
Rows 13 & 14	Med. Green	Blue Green	Gray Check
Row 15	Med. Green	Blue Green	Med. Blue
Rows 16 & 17	Olive Green	Blue Green	Med. Blue
Rows 18 & 19	Olive Green	Blue Green	Blue Green
Row 20	Olive Green	Blue Green	Darker Green
Row 21	Olive Green	Darker Green	Darker Green

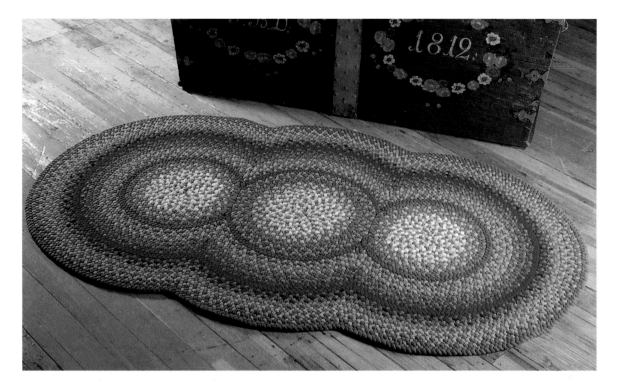

Heather Roses
3'4" x 5'8" (103 x 173 cm)

Color Plan

Rows 1-6	Lt. Olive Green	Lt. Pink	Olive Tweed
Rows 7 & 8	Lt. Olive Green	Brick Red	Olive Tweed
Row 9	Med. Olive Green	Brick Red	Olive Tweed
Rows 10 & 11 (on center circle only)	Med. Olive Green	Taupe	Olive Tweed
Row 12 (rattailed into vs where circles join)	Med. Olive Green	Med. Olive Green	Med. Olive Green
Remaining rows are butted			
Row 13	Med. Olive Green	Taupe	Dusty Rose
Rows 14 & 15	Brick Red	Taupe	Dusty Rose
Row 16	Brick Red	Taupe	Maroon Tweed
Row 17	Brick Red	Gray/Maroon Tweed	Maroon Tweed
Row 18	Old Red	Gray/Maroon Tweed	Maroon Tweed
Row 19	Old Red	Old Red	Old Red
Row 20	Old Red	Brick Red	Dk. Tweed
Row 21	Taupe	Brick Red	Dk. Tweed
Row 22	Taupe	Brick Red	Pink/Gray Tweed
Row 23	Lt. Olive Green	Brick Red	Pink/Gray Tweed
Row 24	Lt. Olive Green	Med. Olive Green	Pink/Gray Tweed
Row 25	Lt. Olive Green	Med. Olive Green	Med. Olive Green
Row 26	Med. Olive Green	Med. Olive Green	Med. Olive Green

My Valentine
30" x 40" (77 x 103 cm)

Color Plan

Rows 1-5	Dusty Rose	Med. Mauve	Multi-Colored Stripe
Row 6	Dusty Rose	Lt. Mauve	Multi-Colored Stripe
Rows 7 & 8	Dusty Rose	Lt. Pink	Multi-Colored Stripe
Rows 9 & 10	Pink	Lt. Pink	Multi-Colored Stripe
Row 11	Pink	Lt. Mauve	Multi-Colored Stripe
Row 12	Dusty Rose	Lt. Mauve	Maroon Plaid
Row 13	Dusty Rose	Dk. Mauve	Maroon Plaid
Row 14	Dk. Mauve	Dk. Mauve	Maroon Plaid

Favorite Colors
36" x 47" (92.5 x 120.5 cm)

Color Plan

Rows 1-3	Silver Gray	Lt. Blue	Lt. Blue
Row 4	Silver Gray	Lt. Blue	Dusty Rose
Row 5	Med. Gray	Lt. Blue	Dusty Rose
Row 6	Med. Gray	Med. Blue	Dusty Rose
Row 7	Med. Gray	Med. Blue	Med. Blue
Row 8	Med. Gray	Med. Blue	Dusty Rose
Rows 9 & 10	Med. Gray	Lt. Blue	Dusty Rose
Row 11	Lt. Blue	Lt. Blue	Dusty Rose
Row 12	Lt. Blue	Lt. Blue	Med. Blue
Row 13	Lt. Blue	Med. Blue	Med. Blue
Row 14	Navy Blue	Med. Blue	Med. Blue
Row 15	Navy Blue	Navy Blue	Navy Blue

Watermelon
18" x 25" (46 x 64 cm)

Color Plan

Rows 1-5	Solid Red
Rows 6-8	Red with Black Seeds
Row 9	Solid Red (rattail)
Row 10	1 Red, 2 Greenish White (butted)
Row 11	Solid Greenish White (butted)
Row 12	Solid Dk. Green (butted)

Santa Fe Strip
22" x 40" rectangle (56.5 x 102.5 cm)

Color Plan

Row 1	Turquoise	Turquoise	Gray Plaid
Row 2	Turquoise	Silver Gray	Gray Plaid
Row 3	Turquoise	Silver Gray	Silver Gray
Row 4	Turquoise	Turquoise	Silver Gray
Row 5	Turquoise	Turquoise	Turquoise
Row 6	Turquoise	Turquoise	Rust
Row 7	Turquoise	Camel	Rust
Row 8	Camel	Camel	Rust
Row 9	Camel	Camel	Camel
Row 10	Camel	Camel	Rust
Row 11	Camel	Turquoise	Gray Plaid
Rows 12 & 13	Turquoise	Turquoise	Gray Plaid
Row 14	Turquoise	Turquoise	Turquoise

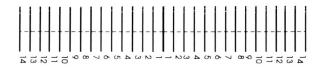

Designer: **Dawn Rapchinski**

Photographer: Paul Jacobs of Charles Studio

Dawn Rapchinski, a rug braider from Ephrata, Pennsylvania, enjoys bringing a craft from Lancaster County's past, rich heritage into the present day. She believes braided rugs symbolize family life. She learned to braid when she wanted a rug for her dining room. Now her successful cottage business provides her the opportunity to work at home with her family. While smaller braided rugs are for sale from her home, she specializes in custom-braiding, especially of room-size rugs for clients.

She is excited by each rug she makes. Dawn believes that when strips of color, tweed, or plaid are braided and laced together, they take on a unique character that creates a special look and warmth for a home.

Top:
Jeans Again, 2' x 3' (61.5 x 92.5 cm)

Bottom:
Peaceful Meadow, 9'3" x 12'3" (2.9 x 3.8 m)

Top:
Mellow Joy, 11' x 14' (3.4 x 4.3 m)

Bottom:
Maroon Harmony, 8'11" x 10'8" (2.5 x 3.3 m)

Designer: **Irene Ford**

Photographer: Russell McDougal

Growing up in rural Kansas, Irene Ford can recall the stock market crash of 1929 and the dust storms of the 1930s. Her mother saved her family's worn cotton clothing and used them to braid and crochet rugs.

After graduating from college, Irene tried her hand at braiding rugs using her own worn clothing. During the next 20 years teaching instrumental music in Boulder, Colorado where she and her husband and two sons lived, Irene continued to braid. She finally considered a rug worthy of entry in the Boulder County Fair and won a blue ribbon.

After retiring from teaching in 1977, Irene decided to work on her braiding in a serious way. She teaches a few students, and makes special order rugs for a limited clientele. Her rugs have been displayed in several shows throughout Colorado.

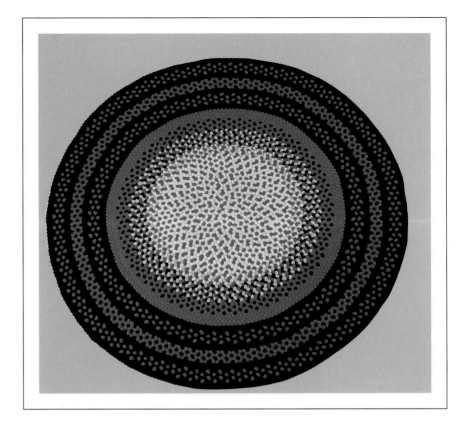

Top:
Braided circle rug

Bottom:
Hooked rug with braided border

Top:
Braided
scalloped rug

Bottom:
Braided
rectangular
rug

Nancy Young has been braiding off and on for more than 30 years. What began as a hobby, evolved into a full-time profession in the mid-80s. With New England roots on her father's side going back to the 1600s, Nancy feels her passion for braiding comes naturally because rug braiding began in the early 1800s in that region of the country.

Nancy has become so skilled at her craft that she is one of only three rug braiders juried by the Pennsylvania Guild of Craftsman. Her work is both displayed and sold in several museums, including the Museum of American Folk Art in New York City.

A math instructor by profession, Nancy enjoys teaching the techniques of braiding to others, too. She makes rugs on commission and repairs damaged antique floor coverings. She resides in Quakertown, Pennsylvania.

Top:
Hexagon rug, 35" (90 cm) diameter

Bottom:
Scalloped rug, 55" (141 cm)

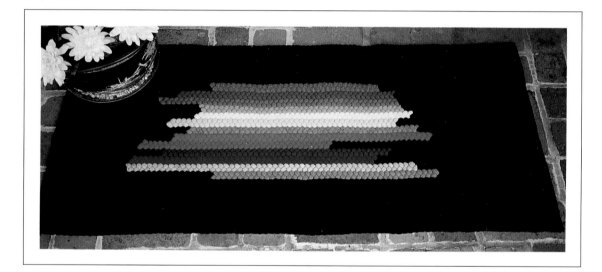

Top:
Navajo rug, 35" x 60" (90 x 152 cm)

Middle:
Spectrum runner, 21" x 48" (54 x 123 cm)

Bottom:
Chair pads, 14" (36 cm) diameter

Designer: **Janice Jurta**

Photographer: Martha Mae Emerson

Janice Jurta owns Country Braid House in Tilton, New Hampshire, a thriving business started as a part-time hobby by her father-in-law, George Jurta, who died in 1986. Country Braid House makes and sells high-quality braided rugs. A former administrative assistant and legal secretary, Janice began working in the shop in 1985; her designs and marketing ideas have helped the business increase its production from two rugs a month to three or more a week.

The rugs are made partly by the machines her father-in-law, George Jurta, designed and patented in 1968. The cutting machine cuts and folds the woolen strips, and the winding machine winds the strips onto bobbins that fit into the braiding machine. Janice's employees hand-lace the braids together.

Most Country Braid House rugs are custom-designed, and the wool comes primarily from New Hampshire firms. Janice also sells kits for making small rugs.

Top:
Williamsburg, 5-1/2' x 7-1/2' (1.7 x 2.3 m)

Bottom:
Forget-Me-Not, 31" x 45" (79.5 x 115.5 cm)

Top:
Log Cabin, 7-1/2' (2.3 m) round

Bottom:
Jefferson, 8-1/2' x 10-1/2'
(2.6 x 1.2 m)

Designer: **LouAnn Mohrman**

Photographer: Mike Keller

LouAnn Mohrman lives in Colcord, West Virginia, and began braiding in 1974. She has participated in numerous national shows and exhibits since 1975, and has won several Merit Awards from Exhibit 60 and the West Virginia Juried Exhibit. LouAnn teaches rug braiding classes at the Monongalia Art Center in Morgantown, and for Elderhostel at the John C. Campbell Folk School in Murphy, North Carolina.

LouAnn enjoys exploring nontraditional forms, such as her wall hanging of a large brown-eyed Susan and her "quilt," (*Granny Squares*) using 12 braided squares laced together with a solid color border. She sells her rugs and mats through the West Virginia Parkways Authority and through commissioned orders.

Top:
Brown Eye, 34" (87.5 cm), wall rug

Bottom:
Good Morning Sun, 28" x 37" (72 x 95 cm), scalloped border

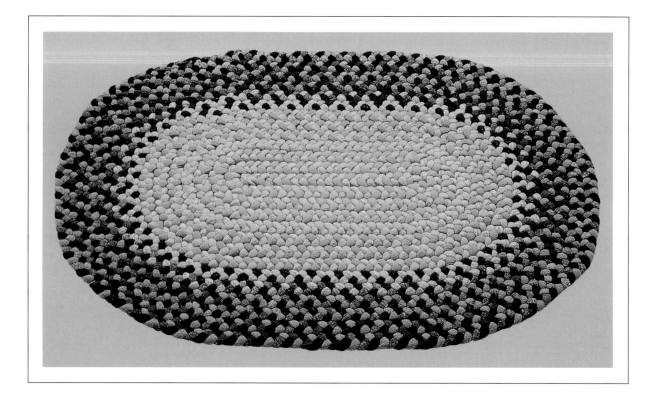

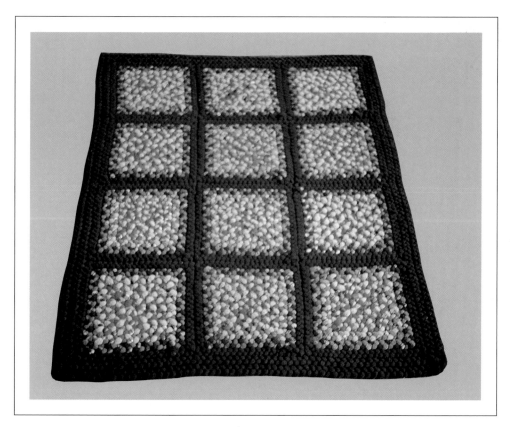

Top:
Joy, 21" x 31" (54 x 79.5 cm)

Bottom:
Granny Squares, 26" x 36" (10 x 92.5 cm). Photographer: LouAnn Mohrman

Designer: **Marjorie N. Dexheimer**

Marjorie Dexheimer, with a B.S. degree in Home Economics as a Related Arts Major, taught in Wisconsin, Michigan, and Connecticut. She received further training in her field, including an advanced crafts for teachers program.

While living in Connecticut, she learned to braid rugs. After moving to Pennsylvania, she joined the Pennsylvania Guild of Craftsmen, and in 1982 was chosen as one of the very few braiders juried by the Pennsylvania Guild of Craftsman. Since 1976, she has taught rug braiding, and has continued to enjoy the interplay of color that braiding invites.

∽

Top:
Turquoise, magenta, and gray oval

Bottom:
Large blue/gray oval

Top:
5-scalloped rug

Bottom:
Blue, green, and gray oval

Designers: **Verna Cox** and **Joan Moshimer**

Verna Cox is very dedicated to the cause of teaching quality rug braiding. She's qualified to do so; a highly skilled and experienced braider, Verna once had a rug of hers displayed in the Smithsonian, and another still hangs in the Maine room of the National 4-H building in Washington, D.C.

A resident of Verona Island, Maine, Verna sells a number of braiding manuals, and has produced several instructional video tapes. Her company, Cox enterprises, also sells braiding kits.

Verna teamed up with one of rug hooking's best-known names, Joan Moshimer, to create a number of rugs that combine intricate hooked patterns with traditional braiding. Until *Rug Hooking Magazine* debuted in 1989, Joan published *Rug Hooker's News and Views* for 18 years. Since then, she has consulted the magazine as contributing editor, providing instructional articles on a regular basis. Joan and her husband, Bob, own and run W. Cushing & Company, manufacturer of Cushing's perfection dyes, with the help of their son, Paul. The three also operate Joan's Rug Hooker Studio, a retail and mail-order supplier of Joan's designs and those of other rug hookers.

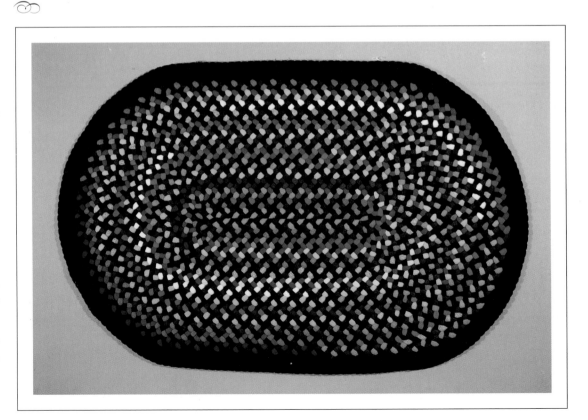

Top:
Olivia Crewel,
24-3/4" x 28"
(63.5 x 72 cm),
hooked center
with braided border

Bottom:
Confetti, 2' x 3'
(61.5 x 92.5 cm)

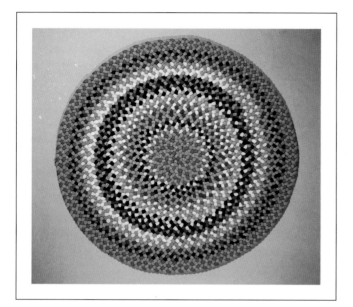

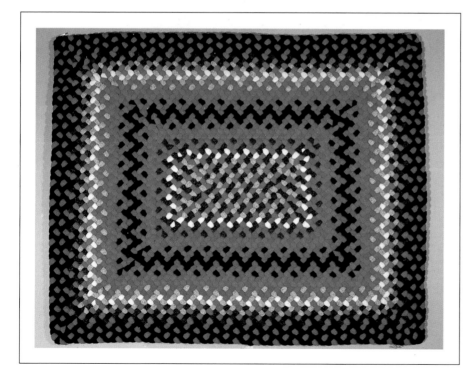

Top left:
Sea Breeze, 30" (77 cm) round

Top right:
Blueberries, 23-1/2" round (60 cm),
hooked center with braided border

Bottom:
Winter Cheer, 2' x 3' (61.5 x 92.5 cm)

Designers: **Marie Griswold** and **Sandra Cheverie**

Photographer: Evan Bracken

Marie Griswold and her daughter, Sandra Cheverie, are long-time rug braiders and designers. Along with other family members, they own and operate Braid-Aid, the well-known company that sells braiding equipment, woolens, and kits, as well as supplies for quilting, shirret, weaving, crewel, and needlepoint.

In 1949, Marie's husband, Roger C. Griswold, watched his wife laboriously braid a rug using the same methods braiders used 100 years ago. He proceeded to invent several braiding devices that help the braider make a rug quicker and more easily. In addition to designing and manufacturing these machines, Braid-Aid operates a wool dyeing plant that produces 39 Palette wool colors, designed by Marie, and exclusive to Braid-Aid. Marie and Sandra live in Pembroke, Massachusetts, where Braid-Aid is located.

Top:
Hooked and braided rug, 43" (110 cm) round, hooked and designed by Hope Camp, braided by Sandra Cheverie

Middle:
Black, gray, and white rectangular rug, 31" x 46" (79.5 x 118 cm), designed by Marie Griswold, braided by Crystal Jones

Bottom:
Blue, purple, and fuschia runner, 31" x 75" (79.5 x 190 cm), designed by Marie Griswold, braided by Carrie Freyermuth

Top:
Red, yellow, green, and black oval rug,
36" x 60" (92.5 x 152 cm),
designed and braided by Marie Griswold

Bottom:
Large red, blue, white, and gold rug,
8-1/2' x 11' (2.6 x 3.3 m),
designed by Marie Griswold,
Sandra Cheverie, and Sandra O'Fihelly,
braided by Sandra O'Fihelly.
Photographer: Orcutt Photography

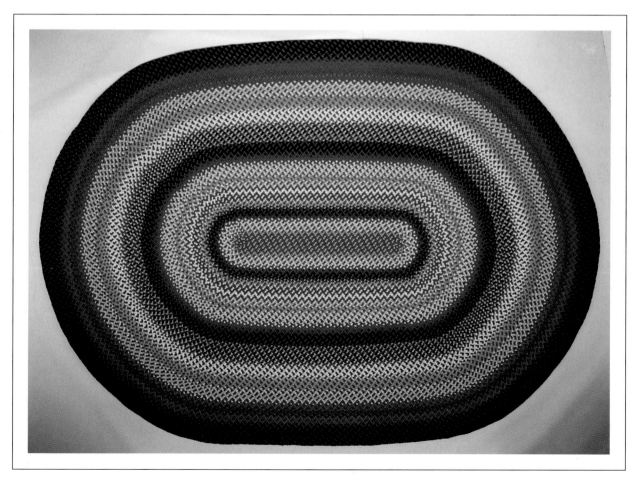

Designer: **Anne Eastwood**

Anne Eastwood's grandmother taught her to braid rugs many years ago. The rugs were actually plaited and sewn together with heavy thread. In 1960, Anne took her first formal lessons from Helen Howard Feeley, the author of *The Complete Book of Rug Braiding*.

Soon Anne began braiding rugs on consignment. Her first dining room rug commission earned her enough money to buy 12 acres of land in the Massachusetts Berkshires where she and her husband had a home built. She taught rug braiding for six years and then moved to Connecticut, where she continued to braid and teach. She managed to keep up these activities even during the busy years of raising five children.

She and her husband retired in 1990 and moved to Lake Placid, Florida, where Anne teaches and works on commissions. After braiding so many round, oval, square, and rectangular rugs, she finds it both exciting and challenging to create new shapes, such as the ones shown here.

Top:
Star, 42" x 42" (107.5 x 107.5 cm)

Middle:
Heart, 38" x 42" (97.5 x 107.5 cm)

Bottom:
Large pig, 19" x 27," (48.5. x 69 cm)

Top:
Triple heart, 3' x 6' (92.5 cm x 1.8 m)

Bottom:
Hooked square/braided scalloped,
33" x 33" (84.5 cm)

Designer: **Sandra Davis**

Sandy Davis has been braiding rugs for about 17 years and has lost track of the number of rugs she has completed. She has taught many people to braid. In this time of throw-away products, she appreciates the value of creating lasting and beautiful rugs braided from new, coat-weight wool.

Top:
Large Hit-or-Miss Rug

Bottom:
Pastel Rug, 26" x 63" (67 cm x 1.5 m)

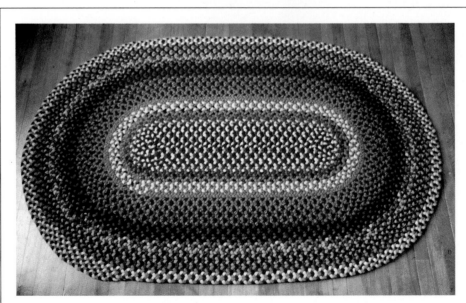

Top:
Red, Blue, Black, and White Rug

Bottom:
Red and Gray Rug, 4' x 7' (1.2 x 2 m)

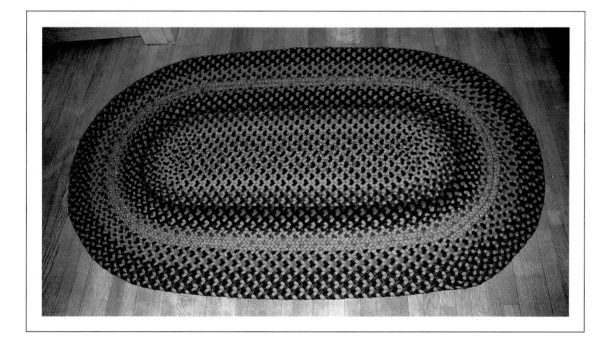

Large pink, turquoise, and black rug, 10' x 13' (3 x 4 m)

Designer: **Doris Rosenberger**

Doris Rosenberger, like other American braiders of previous generations, braids rugs because she appreciates the uniqueness, color, and warmth these rugs provide. She also braids to keep alive a craft handed down to her from her mother.

Although she learned to braid as a child, she did not seriously start braiding rugs until she was 50 years old. She turned to rug braiding initially as a hobby, making rugs for her home and as gifts. Soon she began receiving requests for custom-made rugs. Those first orders grew into her current business, Cottage Braids, located in Telford, Pennsylvania.

Doris really enjoys braiding: it also gives her time to think. In planning a rug, she likes to think about it for a long time before starting. Several times a year she teaches braiding so she can pass on her skill to others.

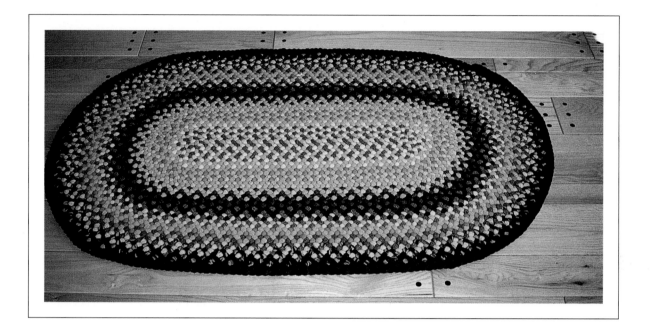

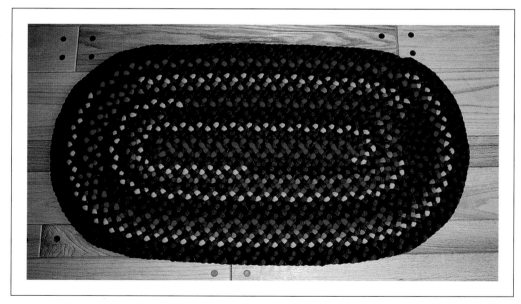

Top:
Small pink, blue, and black rug, 3' x 5' (92.5 x 152.4 cm)

Bottom:
Small black, red, yellow, and blue hit-or-miss, 21" x 38" (54 x 97.5 cm)

Designer: **Jeanette Szatkowski**

Jeanette became a braider in an unusual fashion. She and her husband, Robert, owned a machine shop in Connecticut. Among their customers was Mrs. Harry Fraser, who, after her husband died in 1971, had been running their business, Harry M. Fraser Company, a manufacturer of machines for slitting material used to hook and braid rugs. From time to time, the Szatkowski's repaired Mrs. Fraser's equipment. She and Jeanette became friends, and she taught Jeannette to hook and braid. In 1976, Mrs. Fraser asked the Szatkowski's to take over the making of the cloth slitting machines. A year later she retired completely, and they bought the business, relocating both the machine shop and the retail business to Stoneville, North Carolina.

Jeanette combines braiding and hooking to achieve very appealing results. Her colorful 9-by-14-foot (2.8 x 4.3 m) oval rug was commissioned by a Virginia couple who sent Jeanette samples of the quilting materials she wanted the rug to match.

Top:
Flowers, 24" (61.5 cm)
round, hooked and braided

Bottom:
Multicolored Rug,
6' (1.8 m) round

Neutral-colored Rug, 4' x 6' (1.2 x 1.8 m)

Lesson Plan

▼ ▼ ▼

I have included the following lesson plan for readers interested in teaching rug braiding. This plan has worked for me. It shows the steps needed to finish a rug in six weeks.

Lesson 1

1. Talk about wool, equipment, cost, design, and use of color.

2. Explain how to measure for the size rug you want.

3. Show samples of steps in making the *T*. Pass out practice strips; start braiding the *T*.

4. Pass out Braid-Klamps; talk about Braid-Aids, and distribute, if requested.

5. Practice braiding; teach corner turn, and how to add another strip of wool.

6. Teach how to count five rows.

7. Assignment for next week: Purchase wool, repeat *T*, braid 13 inches (33.5 cm), turn the corner, and braid as much as you can (up to five rows).

Lesson 2

1. Teach center lacing, then teach lacing technique for the rest of the rug.

2. Show how to make a square knot.

3. Teach color change.

4. Assignment for next week: Finish lacing five rows, change color, and continue braiding.

Lessons 3 and 4

1. Check on progress of lacing and other techniques.

2. Continue braiding, lacing, and changing colors.

3. Assignment for next week: Braid and lace ten rows.

4. Be ready to rattail in class at the end of row 15.

Lesson 5

1. Do rattailing.

1. Show how to start butting..

3. Assignment for next week: Start to butt; braid and lace around rug for one or two rows.

Lesson 6

1. Butt one or two rows.

2. Celebrate the students' completion of their rugs. Photograph the rugs.

Wallace Nutting, *A Fairie Tale*

Glossary

Banana-shaped
A rug that isn't straight; both ends curve in one direction.

Band
Several rows of braid using the same color combinations.

Barbells
An oval rug with ends that bulge, the result of skipping on the straight sides before the curve should begin or after the curve should end.

Braid
Three tubes braided together.

Buckling
Not enough skips. This is quite common for beginners. It forces the center of the rug up and the edges up (into a hat shape). The only remedy is to take out the lacing until the rug is flat. Make sure you skip more often when relacing.

Butting
Method of joining the beginning of a row to the end so that it forms a complete circle. This gives the rug a finished look. Usually used for the last two rows. Can be used for all or part of a rug.

Continuous braid
The way almost all rugs are made. Keep braiding, forming a spiral. You braid, lace, change colors, add new strips, and braid again to make the rug larger and larger.

Fold
The side of the tube that has the raw edges turned in towards the center.

Hit-or-miss rug
Braided with small strands of wool of various colors, randomly scattered throughout the rug.

Lacing
Method of attaching the new braid to the body of the rug.

Loop
One of the three tubes after it has been braided.

Pulled loop
After braiding twice overs, the single loop on the opposite side is pulled tightly, therefore called a pulled loop.

Rattailing or tapering
Method of ending a continuous braided rug.

Reverse e
One method of lacing the first row; named because the thread forms an e in reverse.

Row
Three loops braided and laced to a rug.

Scallops
Too many skips make the rug raise up and down. To resolve, don't skip at all on the next row. This will usually flatten it out.

Shoulder
The beginning and end of the curve.

Skip
When lacing on the curved end of the rug (or all around a circle rug), you have to routinely skip one loop on the row you are attaching in order to make a flat, well-shaped rug.

Strand or strip
One length of wool ready to braid.

T-start
The method used to begin the rug.

Tube
A strip of wool after the edges have been turned in.

Twice overs
Braiding twice from one side then once from the other side.

Working braid
The braid you are attaching to the rug.

V
Formed by braiding twice overs in both the top and bottom of heart-shaped rug.

Resources

▼   ▼   ▼

Braid-Aid
466 Washington Street
Pembroke, MA 02359
617-826-2560
617-826-6091
Rug wool, equipment, books, and rug braiding kits
Carry all types of wool, including dyed
Catalog available
Credit cards accepted

Cascade Woolen Mill
3 Dunn Street
P.O. Box 157
Oakland, Maine 04963
207-465-2511
Wool, equipment, and books
Open daily Monday-Saturday; closed January-May
Mail orders all year

Country Braid House
462 Main Street
Tilton, NH 03276
603-286-4511
603-286-4155 (Fax)
Retail shop open Monday-Saturday, 9 am-4 pm, Sunday by appointment
Quality custom-made rugs; many sizes, shapes, and colors

Cox Enterprises
RR 2, Box 245
Fire Road, #22
Verona Island, ME 04416
800-233-0234
207-469-6402
Rug braiding manual
How-to video on braiding
Braiding kits

The Dorr Mill Store
P.O. Box 88
Guild, NH 03754
800-846-3677
603-863-1197
Wool, equipment, and books
Teach rug braiding
Catalog and swatches available

Faribault Woolen Mill Company
1500 Second Avenue NW
P.O. Box 369
Faribault, MN 55021

800-448-9665
507-334-1644
507-334-9431 (Fax)
Rug wool and braiding equipment
Retail, mail/phone order

Harry M. Fraser Co.
433 Duggins Road
Stoneville, NC 27048
Manufacturer of cloth-cutting machines for hooked, braided, and woven rugs
Carry rug wool, equipment, and books
Catalog on request
Mail order

Joan's Rug Hooker Studio
21 North Street
P.O. Box 351
Kennebunkport, ME 04046
800-626-7847
207-967-3520
207-967-8682 (Fax)
Wool, books, equipment for hooking and braiding.
Also Cushing Perfection Dyes

Mandy's Wool Shed
R.R.1, Box 2644
Litchfield, Maine 04350
207-582-5059
Wool by the pound and yard and braiding equipment
Hours: by chance or appointment
Set of samples for a fee

Mill End Store
9701 S.E. McLoughlin Blvd.
Milwaukie, OR 97222
503-786-1234
Retail store: rug wool, braiding supplies, and braiding books
Mail order at P.O. Box 82093, Portland, OR 97282

Osgood Textile Co., Inc.
30 Magaziner Place
Springfield, Mass. 01104
413-737-6488
Retail store
Rug wool by the pound or by the yard

Pendleton Woolen Mills
The Woolen Mill Store
8550 S.E. McLoughlin Blvd.
Portland, OR 97222
503-273-2786
Wide selection of wool and colors
Retail sales store Monday-Saturday, 10 am-5:30 pm
Mail order or by phone
Accept credit cards

Rigby Precision Products
Route 302
P.O. Box 158
Bridgton, Maine 04009
207-647-5679
Sales and service
Manufacturer of cloth-stripping machines for cutting cloth, weaving, braiding, and hooking

Rocky Mountain Rug Crafts
P.O. Box 649
Fredericksburg, TX 78624
210-792-3576
Wool and supplies for braiding and hooking
Mail order
800-331-5213 for phone orders
Accept some credit cards

Spalco Factory Store
21 Pearl Street
Webster, MA 01570
508-949-0406
Retail store open Tues/Wed/Thurs/Sat 10 am-4 pm, Fri 10 am-5 pm
Wool and equipment
Mail/phone orders

Warren of Stafford Mill Store
99 Furnace Avenue
Stafford Springs, CT 06076
203-684-2766
Retail store open Tuesday-Saturday, 10 am-5 pm
Remnant wool

Wooden Nikl
Richard Beauvais-Nikl
11804 Stallion Drive
Pine, CO 80470
303-838-0127
Whale rug braiding stands on order. Send S.A.S.E for price list.

The Woolrich Store
P.O. Box 130 - Park Avenue
Woolrich, PA 17779
717-769-7401
717-769-7832 (Fax)
By bolt, or remnants by pound
Instruction books and equipment
Open Monday-Saturday and Sunday 12 pm-5 pm
Mail/phone orders
Some credit cards honored

The Wool Winder
RR #1
Manilla, Ontario
KOM 250
705-786-1358
Wool and supplies for braiding

Bibliography

Baker, M.E. *Purveyor of Nostalgia—Wallace Nutting's Southbury Connections.* Connecticut: The Newtown Bee, 1984.

Carter, Mary Randolph. *American Family Style.* New York: Viking Studio Books, 1988.

Carty, Sally Clarke. *How to Make Braided Rugs.* New York: McGraw-Hill Book Company, 1977.

Cox, Verna P. *Braided Rug Manual.* Bucksport, Maine: Self-published, 1967.

Feeley, Helen Howard. *The Complete Book of Rug Braiding.* New York: Coward-McCann, Inc., 1957.

Gordon, Beverly. *Shaker Textile Arts.* Hanover, New Hampshire: University Press of New England, 1980.

Horsham, Michael. *The Art of the Shakers.* New Jersey: Chartwell Books, 1989.

Ivankovich, Michael. *The Guide to Wallace Nutting Furniture.* Doylestown, Pennsylvania: Diamond Press, 1990.

Kopp, Joel and Kate. *American Hooked and Sewn Rugs, Folk Art Underfoot.* New York: E.P. Dutton, Inc., 1985.

Lipman, Jean and Winchester, Alice. *The Flowering of American Folk Art (1776-1876).* Pennsylvania: Courage Books, 1974.

Little, Nina Fletcher. *Floor Coverings in New England Before 1850.* Massachusetts: Old Sturbridge Village, 1967.

Manroe, Candace Ord. *Shaker Style, The Gift of Simplicity.* New York: Crescent Books, 1991.

Nutting, Wallace. *Connecticut Beautiful.* Framingham, Massachusetts: Old America Company, 1923.

Rebus, Inc. *American Country, The Needle Arts.* Alexandria, Virginia: Time-Life Books, 1990.

Stockhaus, Peter. *Little Book of Early American Crafts and Trades.* New York: Dover Publications, Inc., 1976.

Tudor, Tasha. *The Dolls' Christmas.* New York: Henry Z. Walck, Inc., 1950.

Weissman, Judith Reiter and Lavitt, Wendy. *Labors of Love, America's Textiles and Needlework, 1650-1930.* New York: Alfred A. Knopf, 1987.

Index